Chance Encounters

Chance Encounters

TALES FROM A VARIED LIFE

Tim Razzall

Biteback Publishing

First published in Great Britain in 2014 by
Biteback Publishing Ltd
Westminster Tower
3 Albert Embankment
London SE1 7SP

ISBN 978-1-84954-753-6

10 9 8 7 6 5 4 3 2 1

A CIP catalogue record for this book is available from the British Library.

Set in Bulmer

Printed and bound in Great Britain by
CPI Group (UK) Ltd, Croydon CR0 4YY

For Matilda and Tom, so they know what happened

CONTENTS

CONTENTS

—CHAPTER ONE—

A CHANCE MEETING

I MET FRANK Sinatra through Robert Maxwell. That's if you can be said to have met someone who was on a private jet with you for fourteen hours and never spoke to you.

I was a partner in a London law firm and was in Paris one Saturday lunchtime in 1988 recovering from a heavy night celebrating the successful completion of a client's acquisition the previous day. As I was checking out of my hotel, Mark Booth rang me. I had known Mark for some years as he had come over from the United States to set up MTV in Europe and we were his lawyers.

He was working for Robert Maxwell and had involved

us in various transactions for the great man. Incidentally, Mark later became the only senior executive to have worked for both Maxwell and Rupert Murdoch when he was hired to run BSkyB and later established for Rupert Murdoch the internet company 'epartners'.

'Mr Maxwell wants you and me to go to Los Angeles to buy MGM for him. There is a meeting at MGM at nine tomorrow morning. Can you get to Los Angeles for that?'

'No way,' I said. 'The last plane leaves London at three and I am still in Paris.'

'Don't worry, get to Stansted by 7 p.m., we are going on the owner's private jet. There is one thing, though; you will have to call Mr Maxwell at five.'

I went back to London, packed and called Mr Maxwell as requested. A familiar voice answered the phone.

'Could I speak to Mr Maxwell please?'

'Who wants him?'

'I'm his lawyer and I understand he wants me to go to Los Angeles for him.'

Robert Maxwell in his inimitable style and voice gave me two clear instructions: 'You are dealing with a fucker and I do not propose to be the fuckee' and 'Your meetings are on the twentieth floor of the MGM building. There is a coin box outside the main entrance. Every hour I want you to come down to the coin box and call me on this number.'

The 'fucker' turned out to be a Mr Kerkorian, the

well-known corporate raider, who had acquired control of MGM. Mark Booth and I were travelling on his private jet. When we arrived at Stansted we were joined by our fellow passengers – Mr and Mrs Kerkorian, Mr and Mrs Sinatra and Frank Sinatra's bodyguard. On the plane there were two double bedrooms and, in the cabin, a number of reclining seats. Mark and I realised we would be in the reclining seats. I had never travelled on a private jet before and quickly grasped why private air travel was an essential tool for the super-wealthy – no airport queues, cramped conditions or contact with ordinary people.

After take-off, dinner was served, during which the Kerkorians and the Sinatras talked to each other and ignored us. Frank Sinatra amused himself by attempting a quick crossword in a magazine he picked up from a rack and then retired to bed. Before going to sleep I picked up his discarded crossword. He had failed with the clue 'Feline animal (3)', c_t.

After seven hours or so we landed at Bangor Maine to clear customs, as the plane did not have the range to go all the way. As the customs official was coming on board, Frank Sinatra came out of his bedroom with a gun in his hand, which he gave to his bodyguard and told him to tuck inside his sock. We then sat and were quizzed by the customs official. After ten minutes or so the bodyguard said to me in a loud and audible voice, 'If this fellow doesn't stop soon Mr Sinatra will have him killed.' This did not seem to speed matters up but eventually the official left and the bedrooms were reoccupied.

As the plane took off, Mark said to me, 'Tim, I've been a Republican all my life but if that man is President Reagan's friend I am voting Democrat next time.' From what I had seen I shared his antipathy.

The rest of the trip was an anticlimax. We checked into the Beverly Wilshire Hotel in Beverly Hills and left for the meeting.

We reported to Mr Maxwell every hour from the coin box. The meeting lasted only until the early afternoon. We agreed an in-principle deal to buy for $500 million, went back to the Beverly Wilshire to shower, and flew back to London that evening by more orthodox means.

The purchase never took place. It became clear that Robert Maxwell never intended to buy the company. It was a publicity stunt because Rupert Murdoch had just announced his purchase of 20th Century Fox, and the newspapers he controlled were full of him buying MGM.

In any event, as we subsequently discovered, he wouldn't have had the money – presumably too much to steal from the pension fund.

Not long afterwards a French entrepreneur bought MGM for a lot more than we had negotiated.

But I did get to meet Frank Sinatra.

I suppose I had received an indication some years earlier that Robert Maxwell was not entirely to be trusted. It
was a matter of public record that a Department of Trade
and Industry inquiry in 1971 into the affairs of Pergamon
Press had found that 'he was not a person who can be
relied upon to exercise proper stewardship of a public
company'. But the law firm of which I became a partner
witnessed a more private hint of his dishonesty.

On this occasion we were acting for an entrepreneur
who was negotiating to sell his business to Maxwell. The
negotiations were tough but agreement was finally reached
one evening. The meeting was in Maxwell's office and the
proposed agreement that had been circulated earlier had
many manuscript amendments. 'Don't worry,' said Maxwell, 'you boys go off to dinner, come back in an hour or
so and my secretary will have produced a clean document
for signature.' When the lawyers came back my colleague
had the presence of mind to insist on reading the agreement. All the negotiated amendments had been included
save one. Maxwell had altered the price for the company
in his favour, so he was paying less than had been verbally
agreed. When challenged about this he blamed the typist
for making a mistake. But the expression on his face was
that of the eight-year-old boy whose mother had found
him stealing money from her purse to buy sweets.

Fortunately, my dealings with Maxwell's organisation

over the years were restricted to his video and broadcasting business, so I did not have any clue about his theft from the pension funds, which many say precipitated his death. But I never forgot the crispest instruction any lawyer has received: that his client did not propose to be the fuckee.

As a later coda to my dealings with Robert Maxwell, long after his death I found myself sitting at lunch next to his widow's former personal assistant. She confirmed a number of things to me about him. First, the rumours that he was not the Czech Jan Hoch he said he was and was in fact a Russian substitute were not true. She had travelled with him to the Czech village in which he claimed to have been brought up and he clearly recognised details of the village that he could have known only if he came from there. Second, the rumours about his death were untrue. Whatever his financial problems he would never have killed himself, nor, as was rumoured at the time, would Mossad have murdered him. The relationship was too close. She believed the truth was prosaic. Simply an accident, with him falling overboard after drinking too much.

—CHAPTER TWO—

EARLY LIFE

MY EXPERIENCE WITH Frank Sinatra demonstrates why I would answer David Copperfield's first question in the negative. I do not regard myself as the hero of my own life. My luck has been in chance encounters with people in different walks of life – politicians, lawyers, businessmen, sportsmen. I agree with Haruki Murakami that chance encounters are what keep us going.

So bearing that in mind, I have never thought a person's early life was relevant to their later success. I never agreed that Julius Caesar's treatment of the pirates as a young boy demonstrated the inevitability of his later triumphs.

I never accepted the idea that Margaret Thatcher's economic policy was a direct result of Alderman Roberts's retail economics. For me, Abraham Lincoln said it all in 1860: 'It is a great piece of folly to attempt to make anything out of my early life.'

Nevertheless, for everyone, early experiences contain some seeds of later development.

My early years can be swiftly summarised. I was born in 1943 to Muriel and Leonard Humphrey Razzall. The origin of the name 'Razzall' has often been questioned. The family can be traced back to the eighteenth century in Dorking in Surrey. Indeed, on the wall of Dorking Cricket Club in the shadow of Box Hill there used to be a framed scorecard of a nineteenth-century match in which a Razzall was playing.

I have always assumed that there are two possibilities: either the Razzalli family settled in Surrey from Italy in the sixteenth or seventeenth century and the 'i' got dropped; or poor spelling in parish records converted 'Russell' to 'Razzall'. I have always preferred the former version and justify the waving of my hands when speaking and my tactility as the result of my Italian origins. Pronunciation of the name has changed with the generations. My father emphasised the second syllable whereas my brother and I do not.

As it has been put to me, 'So it's Razzall as in dazzle not Razzall as in fuck all.'

In recent years my name has caused mirth among the journalist community. When I became a life peer, George Parker welcomed me in the *Financial Times* as the only peer who has ever taken his title from a pornographic magazine. I fear Tom Baldwin's epithet in *The Times* has stuck – 'Lord Razzall, known as Lord Razzall of Dazzle for his love of the high life'. Unfair but witty! The 'Black Dog' column in the *Mail on Sunday* did go too far in suggesting that Charles Kennedy's drinking problems were provoked by having me as his friend, as I was known as the 'Cocktail Shaker'. When I protested to the journalist who wrote the column that I never drank cocktails and had certainly not served them to Charles, he claimed that he had been on holiday when the piece was written.

I suppose a clue to the Razzall origins might have been given to me by an orthodontist I sat next to at a dinner in my twenties. I asked her to recommend a dentist, which she did after telling me never to trust an Australian. She held my chin in her hand and asked me to open my mouth. She expressed surprise that unlike most Englishmen I did not have an Indo-European jaw. So maybe that makes us Mongolian.

A more outlandish suggestion was made to my daughter, Katie, some years ago. She found herself at dinner sitting next to a medical consultant, who, when she told him her name, asked her whether she was anything to do with the 'Travelling Razzalls'.

Apparently a traveller with our name had been admitted to hospital to be treated by him. After a visit from her family, all the moveable equipment from the room had disappeared. Apparently he had told her that if the equipment in the room was not returned by his next visit she would be discharged from the hospital. It was. So perhaps we are of Roma origin.

We do know that the Razzalls left Surrey in the nineteenth century, when the new Archbishop of York took my great-grandfather, who was his gardener, to look after the garden at Bishopthorpe Palace in York. My grandfather Razzall moved to Scarborough as a primary school teacher, where he remained all his adult life, and my father was born there.

Landscape gardening was also in the family tradition on my paternal grandmother's side. Sally Thompson was born in Scarborough in 1882, the youngest of ten children. Her father designed Scarborough cemetery, a place of Victorian splendour, although not, I believe, the cemetery from which Jimmy Savile's gravestone was recently removed. Her great-great-grandfather had marched with Bonnie Prince Charlie in 1745 and deserted the Young Pretender before he reached Derby, making his way east to settle in Scarborough. This probably explains my ability to sing Jacobite songs as a party piece.

My father went to Scarborough Boys' High School and met my mother in Scarborough as a teenager. He had impressed a visiting luminary from London in a school debating competition, and said luminary persuaded my grandfather to let him come to London to train as a solicitor. This was not cheap in the early 1930s. No salary was paid to the articled clerk and eighty pounds' stamp duty had to be paid on the deed of articles. It took many years for this to be abolished due to pressure from the backwoodsmen of the profession, who feared that the floodgates would open and let the wrong sort of people become solicitors! Somehow my grandfather found the money and my father came to London.

Sadly, it emerged that his principal's interest in him was more sexual than professional, so he was forced to transfer his articles to Frank, later Sir Frank Medlicott, who became a National Liberal MP after the split in the Liberal Party over the formation of the coalition in the early 1930s.

My parents married in 1935 after my father qualified as a solicitor, four years before the outbreak of war. I suspect that children either absorb or reject the political views of their parents. In my case it was clearly the former. My father had been involved in Liberal Party politics from an early age. At the outbreak of war he was the prospective parliamentary candidate for Finchley, but for the 1945 election he switched constituencies and fought Scarborough, where he came a credible second to the Tory winner.

I asked once why he was a Liberal. 'Oh, my grandfather taught me to hate the Tories because Tory landlords on the Yorkshire moors evicted tenants in the 1880s if they voted Liberal.' I suspect my father would not have approved of the 2010 Tory–Liberal Democrat coalition.

His political life had to end when he accepted a judicial appointment as a Taxing Master in the early 1950s. But his interest remained and as a boy my chance encounters started early when I met various Liberal luminaries in our house.

We lived in a semi-detached mock Tudor house close to Acton Town station in west London, with four bedrooms, two reception rooms and a sizeable kitchen. I suppose our life was typical of middle-class families of that era. My father went to work every day, I went to school and my mother stayed at home. I was already twelve years old when my brother Charles was born. Like many families, we obtained our first television set in 1953 to watch the coronation – from then on, a small black-and-white screen in a box sat in the corner of the living room. But radio still played a large part in our lives. I was gripped as a boy by the serial *Journey into Space* and always listened to *The Archers*, in those days at 6.45 p.m. Indeed, I was actually listening to Grace's last words of love to Phil

Archer as she died in the episode put on by the BBC as a spoiler for the launch of ITV in 1955.

The house was large enough to entertain when my parents were in the mood to do so. The young Jeremy Thorpe was highly amusing to a teenager. Basil Wigoder (later Lord Wigoder) and his wife Yolande were particularly kind to me, probably, as I later discovered from Yolande, because my parents had introduced them. This was the generation who kept the Liberal Party going when it was on the brink of extinction after the 1951 election.

It was not only Liberal politicians I encountered. When in private practice, my father had been attracted to the raffish world of the Chelsea Arts Club and had been instructed by a number of well-known artists. Rodrigo Moynihan was the most prestigious, as Professor of Painting at the Royal College of Art. He was married to Elinor Bellingham-Smith, who specialised in portraits set in the East Anglian countryside. She was commissioned to paint me as an eight-year-old boy, presumably in lieu of fees. I remember being taken by my mother to sit for Elinor in Chelsea. I had never been to Chelsea or to such a large house. I remember a searingly cold room and an attractive middle-aged woman who smelt of paint. But my most significant memory is of being given steak for lunch. Rationing was still in force and I had certainly never had steak before. I can remember that it was so tough as to be virtually inedible, and not just because I had children's teeth. Lack of interest in steak has stayed with me. But the portrait of the solemn young boy with Don Bradman's book on cricket on his lap, which has travelled with me to wherever I have lived, is a reminder to me of that experience.

John Minton was another story. My father had represented him in various disputes and had become a friend. For a number of years he had been the tutor to the painting school at the Royal College of Art. By the mid-1950s he was clearly seriously alcoholic and in 1955 my father decided that he should come to stay with us to ensure he did not drink himself to death. So at the age of twelve I was sharing our house in Ealing with an obviously gay alcoholic, in the days when homosexuality was still illegal. In the summer my ebullient father had a party in the garden with cardboard cut-outs painted by the great man stuck round the lawn. I remember my parents in fancy dress as King Arthur and Queen Guinevere, and being embarrassed at my father's eccentric behaviour. In her biography of John Minton, Frances Spalding alleges that my father kept him as virtually a prisoner in our house against his will, which was certainly not true. In any event, he left after a few months and gave my mother a watercolour painted in Switzerland, which I still have. He committed suicide in 1957.

John Minton was not the only person through whom I witnessed the perils of alcoholism as a boy. Robert Crust was my father's cousin, whose mother my father had lodged with when he first came to work in London. Her husband had been a barrister's clerk, one of whose members of chambers became Lord Chancellor. Robert was unmarried and kept losing his job as a solicitor, I now realise through drink. I do remember one evening when he came to supper. I suppose I was about six or seven, and I had a clockwork toy with suction feet that moved up and down a wall. When I left the table and fixed the toy to the wall behind him, Robert screamed as the toy moved slowly upwards and ran from the room. My mother explained that he had an illness called DTs. At the time I found the incident amusing, but when I grew up I realised it was delirium tremens, a serious alcoholic symptom.

At an early age my father introduced me to cards, a skill that, like riding a bicycle, never leaves you. A group of his friends met in our house every Friday evening to play solo whist for money. Solo is a great gambling game where you bid to make five tricks – solo; no tricks – misère; nine tricks – abundance; and all thirteen tricks – abundance declare. Each player puts money in the pot on each deal until one person has a winning hand. As in bridge or whist, each player has to follow the suit lead. The player with the highest bid plays against the other three players and wins the

pot with misère, abundance or abundance declare. From
the age of ten or so I waited nervously to see if everyone
arrived. If one of his friends did not appear I stood in, an
event that occurred regularly.

So by the age of sixteen I was pretty proficient. I still
feel a source of shame at my behaviour on my first skiing
holiday with the school. We went by train and ferry to
Switzerland and as we pulled out of Victoria station an
older boy said he was putting together a solo whist school
and would I like to play. I asked him with an innocent
expression to explain the rules as I had never played before.
Oh dear. I fear I won enough money over the next few
hours to fund my holiday. Beginner's luck, the others pre-
sumed. I felt a sense of shame.

Incidentally, it was on that holiday that I suffered my
first ever hangover. I was given Cointreau, drank far too
much and was violently sick. Even the smell of it today
makes me retch.

My earliest childhood memory, of which my family are
sceptical, was of the V2s coming over London in spring
1945, and being taken in a pram by my mother to see the
large hole where a V2 had landed in nearby Gunnersbury
Park. But I certainly have childhood memories of my first
year at school – Lionel Road Primary School, next to Gunnersbury Park, still visible from the elevated section of
the M4 en route to Heathrow Airport. My first class had

fifty children and was taught by the elderly Miss Lidstone, who had turned mixed-ability teaching into an art form.

Bullying was rife. I remember defending one poor boy who had bright ginger hair and was ostracised for dropping ginger-coloured shit down his leg from an attack of diarrhoea. I particularly remember another boy. His father had been sent to prison and his poverty-stricken mother had to send him to school in his father's boots. At break, various boys said that Victor couldn't play in our game of football wearing those boots as they feared for their shins. I said that if Victor wasn't playing nor was I. So Victor played. Unknown to me the incident was being witnessed by our formidable head teacher Miss Hattersley, who gave me sixpence and told me I was a good boy.

All of the boys at school supported Brentford Football Club, which was ten minutes away from the school, in Griffin Park. Planning permission has now been given for a new stadium even closer to the school, in Lionel Road itself. In those days Brentford played in the old Second Division, now the Championship, to which the club has recently returned.

I will always remember the date George VI died in 1952, as that was the day I attended my first Brentford game. My mother was to take me and when I woke the announcement was made on the radio that the King had died. I spent the morning in trepidation that the game would be cancelled. Far from it. The players wore black armbands, a one-minute silence ensued and the game proceeded as planned. They did these things differently in those days! My mother did have difficulty explaining to me what the word 'fucking' meant when used generally as an adjective from the terraces behind us, either about the referee or an unfortunate Brentford player who had made a mistake. When I asked her how 5,000 men could get off work on a weekday afternoon she gave me a strange look and told me that I would understand when I was older.

Over the next few years I went often to Brentford with chums. I saw the great Stanley Matthews play on the right wing and as we boys stood at the front by the touchline for half the game, as he was on our side of the pitch, we could almost touch him, which was more than Brentford's hapless left back did. I saw Derek Dooley play for Sheffield Wednesday in the season he rivalled Dixie Dean for the record number of goals scored in a league season. Sadly he was injured later and had to have his leg amputated. Brentford even signed Tommy Lawton, the old England centre forward, in the twilight of his career.

When my father was in private practice as a solicitor, he had often briefed the QC Frank Soskice, later to be Home Secretary in Harold Wilson's first government. He asked Frank Soskice where to send me to school, and he suggested his old school, St Paul's.

So in 1952 I left Lionel Road and started at Colet Court, St Paul's junior school, located in the Hammersmith Road. The buildings are still there, just before Brook Green, but were turned into flats when the senior and junior schools moved to Barnes in the 1960s. London was still recovering from the war, with holes in the ground where buildings had been destroyed by German bombs. With hindsight, so were some of the staff. Mr Wormald had difficulty keeping order and malicious boys said this was because he had been tortured in a Japanese prisoner-of-war camp. Mr Hardy, known by all as Horace, had fought, we believed, with Monty in north Africa, and had breath smelling of beer in the afternoons after his liquid lunches in the Red Cow pub opposite.

Lessons learnt early tend to stay for life. With Mr Berry I developed a love of history and literature. He also caught me in an act of blatant plagiarism. I was an avid reader of G. A. Henty, who had written historical novels for the Victorian boy. I had recently finished *With Clive in India* and for my weekly history essay simply copied out passages from the Henty novel. When my essay was returned I was given 19 out of 20 and the comment 'With Clive in India?'. To this day I have no idea how he knew.

The master we most feared was Mr Robinson, known to all as 'Robo'. Small and rotund, he taught the bottom stream and ruled them with a rod of iron, once striking a misbehaving boy over the head with a cricket bat. In my early days I can remember being so terrified when he shouted at me that I weed down my trouser leg.

But my overwhelming recollection of Robo is as an umpire on the cricket field. The Colet Court under-12s were playing Royal Masonic School's under-12s, who batted first. When the ninth wicket fell they had not scored a run, and Robo was beside himself with excitement. I was bowling at number 11 from his end. When I hit the batsman on the pad he was closer to the square leg umpire than to the stumps, but Robo gave him out leg before wicket, although no one had appealed and he was clearly not out as the ball could not possibly have hit the wicket. So Royal Masonic School were out for nought and we made it to the front page of the London *Evening News* the next day.

I of course have a clear recollection of other masters. Nigel Chawner taught Latin and Greek and became a friend for life. Kenneth Langsford took the top form as well as the First XI cricket. Alex Alexander was the music master. In light of the recent allegations against him of sexual abuse of boys in *The Times* newspaper, I should say that I had no evidence of impropriety by him against me or any of my friends – and little boys do talk to each other. I suppose looking back he was rather effeminate – he reeked of cologne – but at the time I just felt he was a nice man.

Colet Court was a happy place – intellectually

stimulating, providing sporting opportunities and encouraging creative behaviour. I can still smell the make-up on
my face from my performances as Hotspur in *Henry IV,
Part I* and Bottom in *A Midsummer Night's Dream.*

Colet Court was on the north side of the Hammersmith Road, which was not the busy thoroughfare it is
today. I remember at the age of ten walking to Hammersmith Tube station with my nose in a book. So engrossed
was I that I turned left to cross Hammersmith Broadway
still reading. A screech of tyres alerted me to how close I
had been to disaster.

In 1957, I crossed the Hammersmith Road to join the
senior school. The imposing red-brick building had been
built in the mid-nineteenth century in the style of the Royal
Courts of Justice or St Pancras Station, with the playing
fields at the back stretching to the Cromwell Road.

When the school moved to Barnes in the late 1960s, the
building was demolished, an outrageous act of architectural vandalism. The only surviving building is the old high
master's house, soon to become a restaurant. I still cannot drive towards London over the Hammersmith flyover
without a pang of nostalgia for my youth in the building
on the left long gone.

At St Paul's I received an education that had changed
little since the 1850s; indeed, some might say from the date
of foundation of the school in 1509. One week, all Latin,

one week, all Greek, relieved only by a weekly period of ancient history. Little wonder that ten out of the twelve boys in my form obtained Oxford scholarships or exhibitions. A number of my class went on to future success. Paul Lever became Sir Paul Lever as our ambassador to Berlin. Bernard Rix abandoned his dream of the Tory Cabinet to become Lord Justice Rix in the Court of Appeal. John Govett rose through Schroders merchant bank to be a hugely successful fund manager.

As I gave up Latin and Greek to read law at Oxford almost fifty years ago, the content of my education has long faded. But memories of those who taught me will never die. For some reason, at St Paul's what would elsewhere have been called the sixth form was known as the eighth form. The classical eighth was run by two legendary teachers, whose personalities could not have been more different.

Pat Cotter taught Greek. Grey haired and usually in a light-coloured suit, reeking of cologne, he epitomised flamboyance. Outside his teaching life he was captain of the British croquet team and the bridge correspondent at the *Financial Times*. Boys who were not participating in lunchtime sports were introduced to lunchtime bridge with Pat Cotter. Although the substance has gone, I remember the enthusiasm for Sophocles, Euripides and Aeschylus with which he endowed countless generations.

Dr Cruickshank, the Latin master, was Pat Cotter's

opposite, and rather taciturn, but when he spoke you certainly listened. He was in charge of the school Combined Cadet Force (CCF), which I joined believing it would prepare me for National Service, though in fact that was abolished in 1959, halfway through my school life. I still recall an early lesson. A piece of my military clothing had been stolen from my locker and I was pretty sure who had stolen it. When I went to Dr Cruickshank to report the theft and shop the miscreant, I received a serious dressing down and was told it was my responsibility to ensure I had my clothing at all times, and no he was not going to accept an excuse that someone had stolen it.

Cruickers had a guttural r. This emanated from the back of his throat, not in the style of Roy Jenkins or the Marquess of Salisbury, who, on Prime Minister Eden's resignation, interviewed members of the Cabinet, inviting a choice between Butler and Macmillan with the memorable phrase, 'Which is it to be, Wab or Hawald?' I can still hear his use of the letter 'r' when describing Propertius as the tenderest of the Latin love poets. It was from Cruickers that we learnt a skill I practise to this day. Do your best creative work first thing in the morning and your best learning later in the evening; things learnt last thing at night are better retained in your brain.

The third master in the classical eighth who taught us ancient history arrived as a master at the school on the same day I arrived as a pupil. Christopher Train had come from Oxford after National Service so was probably ten years older than me. It is not uncommon for teenage boys to make heroes of older boys or young masters. There is nothing sexual about it. It is just that you crave your hero's company and hang on his every word. Chris Train was undoubtedly my hero. He lived in Ealing, quite close to our home, and it was a red letter day if I happened to meet him on the Tube. This meant twenty minutes of conversation with just me. Once when he invited me to go with him to the British Museum after school I was almost sick with excitement.

We learnt a lot about life from young masters like Chris Train. Once, as we were coming towards the holidays, the cricket XI had been out for an end-of-term party. The next morning we had a double period of ancient history where we were set an essay. After about thirty minutes my friend Richard East complained that such was his hangover he could not complete the assignment and indeed was about to be sick. Chris Train erupted and gave Richard a dressing down in front of the whole class: 'Let me give you a lesson in life. However much you drink you must always be ready and on parade the next morning.'

Some years later, to the school's surprise, Chris left teaching to join the civil service. He rose to be in charge of the prison service. His career foundered when he was

unfairly blamed for the prison riot in Manchester, with
the Home Secretary refusing to take responsibility. Chris
and his wife moved to Shropshire, where, sadly, he died
of cancer a few years back. Although I have long left my
school days behind there is a bit of me that still remem-
bers him as a hero.

During my time at St Paul's the high master was
Anthony Gilkes, for some reason known to all as 'Trickle'.
A somewhat austere man, he came from a classical background and indeed taught my form the New Testament
in Greek.

The memory that sticks most vividly in my mind all
these years later is of his behaviour when interviewing senior boys as to their suitability to became a school prefect.
It was well known, as it was handed down by our prede-
cessors, that his final question was always, 'Tell me, what
would you do if you went into the lavatories and saw boys
tossing themselves off in rows?' The acceptable answer
was 'Come and tell you at once, sir.'

Subsequent allegations of sexual impropriety of masters at Colet Court and St Paul's have now extended way
beyond those against Alex Alexander to which I referred
earlier. I was obviously aware of the allegations against
Alan Doggett, who taught music at Colet Court after my
time, and who was forced to resign, and committed suicide
in 1978. He was high-profile as a result of his friendship

with Andrew Lloyd Webber and indeed I believe *Joseph and the Amazing Technicolor Dreamcoat* was first written for performance at Colet Court. I should record that neither I nor any of my friends had any knowledge of or complaints about any master. In my early days, corporal punishment, particularly for boys in the lower forms, still existed. I have no knowledge as to whether any master derived sexual pleasure from administering corporal punishment, as *The Times* has alleged. None of my friends ever complained and, for me, Anthony Gilkes's eccentric question was as far as it ever went.

I cannot leave my school days without touching on my encounters with Field Marshal Montgomery. He had attended the school as a boy and had commandeered the high master's study as his headquarters for the planning of the D-Day invasion in 1944. The plaque commemorating this was on the study wall and has now been moved to the school building in Barnes. Montgomery was a fierce and formidable figure. I remember the school CCF lining up to be inspected by him on a sweltering June day with the temperature pushing 90° Fahrenheit. At least ten boys collapsed like ninepins as he moved slowly down our ranks, and had to be carried off with sunstroke. A more enjoyable occasion was lining up to shake his hand before a First XV rugby match. But my abiding memory is of his idea of small talk to boys. He only had one sentence: 'Get your hair cut, boy.'

By the time I left St Paul's, Monty was chairman of the governors and ensured that his right-hand man in the Eighth Army, Tom Howarth, became high master. Tom's son Alan came into my life much later. Having first been elected as a Tory MP, he crossed the floor to join Labour in 1995 and is now a Labour peer in the House of Lords.

—CHAPTER THREE—

OXFORD UNIVERSITY

WITH MY CLASSICAL education at St Paul's School I had always assumed I was destined for Oxford or Cambridge. In those days, colleges grouped together to set the scholarship examination, and I was entered for the group at Oxford consisting of St John's, Worcester and, from memory, Hertford. Worcester offered me a scholarship and I began there in 1962, not taking the gap year that would become the norm later on.

For most of my contemporaries, Oxford is a place remembered with warm nostalgia. I am not sure we enjoyed it at the time with the warmth given by hindsight. After all, that was where we changed from boys to men, inevitably a somewhat painful process. Of course, the previous year had seen the departure of the last group who came up as fully fledged adults, having completed their two years' National Service. But we were a group of fresh-faced eighteen-year-olds eager to taste what life might have to offer.

Worcester College had traditionally been dominated by boys from the old public boarding schools – no girls until many years later. I recently attended a college reunion of my contemporaries and the Provost, Dick Smethurst, started his welcome speech with the reminder that today 'only half of you would have been here'. But although girls were not admitted until many years later, the public school character of the college was now changing with an influx of boys from the grammar schools of the state sector – comprehensive schools were not yet invented.

Although I spent far too much time on the rugby, football and cricket fields to participate in Oxford politics, I did stand for my first elected office – Secretary of the Junior Common Room – and won. Anthony May, now Sir Anthony May, a Lord Justice of Appeal, was elected President. The next year I stood for President and lost but learnt a fundamental political lesson. My main opponent was involved in Oxford Labour politics and was always going to maximise the ex-grammar school northern vote. Although I didn't share many of their political views, the

ex-boarding school public schoolboys were more or less
for me. Sadly, a third candidate decided to stand whose
constituency was pretty much the same as mine. He came
third but took enough votes from me to stop me winning.
So a key lesson was learnt for later life. You will lose a
first-past-the-post election if the natural vote for you is
split.

A kaleidoscope of memories remain from my Oxford
days. Drinking far too much port and sherry; in those days
no one drank wine. Indeed, to this day I cannot drink a
glass of port; even the smell makes me gag. Being taken
out by Chris Haskins, now Lord Haskins, who later ran
Northern Foods and became Tony Blair's deregulation
czar. For the first and only time in my life I drank anise,
which made my legs buckle. Chris to this day swears he
has never been drunker. As I woke with no hangover or
any other apparent side effect I realised what a dangerous
drink it is and why the French used to ban absinthe. Being
able to sing the whole score of Bernstein's *West Side Story*
with chums without prompting. Playing cricket in The
Parks for the university. In my first year as twelfth man the
legendary Nawab of Pataudi made me sit for six hours in
his new pads to break them in. In my second year I took a
number of wickets against the counties but narrowly failed
to win a blue against Cambridge. Losing the rugby cup-
pers final against Trinity College by a solitary try, scored

by Mike Hogan, who went on to fame as an Olympic ath-
lete. Meeting the elderly philosopher Bertrand Russell at
a friend's house during one vacation. He had come to discuss plans for the Campaign for Nuclear Disarmament, of
which he was a leading proponent. Watching Churchill's
funeral in the college television room and crying when
the cranes along the Thames dipped in tribute as his cof-
fin passed up river. The mists of autumn, the chilliness
of spring, as well as the warm smell of summer grass. In
our case we also had the big freeze of 1963, when snow
and ice paralysed the country for the best part of three
months. Unfortunately for us, the freezing of all lavatory
pipes coincided one night with an attack of food poison-
ing for everyone who had eaten the college dinner. So no
diarrhoea could be flushed away for days.

The college dons were of course integral to our lives.
The legendary Sir John Masterman had just retired as Provost. He appeared from time to time as a shadowy elderly
figure on the touchline supporting a Worcester rugby or
soccer team. It was some years later that we learnt of his
key role during the Second World War as a recruiter of
secret agents and a key player in what became MI6.

Sir John's replacement as Provost was Oliver Franks,
who arrived at the same time as I came up as an undergraduate. Lord Franks came with a fearsome reputation as
diplomat, businessman and academic. I believe he was the

first man to have headed two Oxbridge colleges. As Secretary of the Junior Common Room I had some dealings with the Provost, although his somewhat stiff manner did not immediately endear him to undergraduates. His wife was a much warmer character. Nevertheless, I remember his final advice to me as he shook me by the hand in farewell: 'My advice to you, Tim, is change your job every ten years. That's what I have done and it has served me well.'

He was certainly the man governments turned to if they wanted a detailed inquiry that would not be a whitewash but would not be overcritical.

Harry Pitt was Dean of the college, responsible, I suppose, for our behaviour and moral welfare. I later came to suspect that he had taken on Sir John Masterman's role as a secret agent recruiter, although he never approached me. A modern historian by subject, Harry was good at keeping in touch with former undergraduates of all persuasions, including Rupert Murdoch, who had been at the college reading philosophy, politics and economics in the 1950s. Harry told me years later that when Murdoch was contemplating buying the *Times* and *Sunday Times* newspapers in 1981 he asked Harry for advice. 'I really don't believe the British establishment will let me do this.'

'I am sure they will,' Harry told me he replied. 'They are desperate to keep the newspaper alive.'

I always found Harry easy to deal with, although

Petronella Wyatt suggests that he could be rude and acer-
bic. She alleges that in 1986 she ran away from Worcester
in her second week when, in a tuition class, she fluffed a
French translation and Harry said to her, 'Do you Thatch-
erites not do French or are you just stupid?'

But the most influential figure for me was the young
law tutor Francis Reynolds. His encyclopaedic knowledge,
attention to detail and challenges in argument inspired us
all, as the subsequent success of countless of his pupils
in the two branches of the legal profession provides testament. As an undergraduate and in his subsequent BCL
he had been rivalled by the brilliant South African lawyer
Lennie Hoffman, who went on to fame at the Bar and in
the judiciary. Did Francis actually say to us or did I dream
he said that the only reason Lennie Hoffman got better
marks than him in the BCL was because he was Jewish and
worked over the Christmas holidays? I certainly did not
dream a conversation in my third year when he suggested
I should go to the Bar rather than become a solicitor. I do
not remember the reason I gave him for not changing my
mind. I do remember what I thought: I would never be
good enough on my feet to perform in court. After forty-five
years in politics maybe I was wrong.

It would be inappropriate to leave my school and university days without reference to the cloud that hung over
our family. My father was what in those days was called a

manic depressive, but today would be described as bipolar. Understanding of and sympathy for mental illness was rare. Treatment consisted either of electric shock therapy or drugs that left the patient in a zombie-like condition. Having had electric shock therapy once, my father resisted attempts to have further treatment as he was traumatised by the shocks he had been given.

Only those who have had the experience of a manic depressive relation will understand the impact on family life. Wide mood swings went from manic behaviour to normality and then to depression. With hindsight, the manic episodes were amusing – standing outside our neighbour's house and shouting 'Come out, you queer'; obtaining a meeting with the Lord Chancellor to complain that he was being pursued by Russian spies; and endless extravagance with money.

I was made aware of my father's illness at the age of twelve. Indeed, his behaviour could hardly be hidden from me as I grew up. Until then, my mother had protected me from any awareness of the reality of his illness. When episodes were out of control I was sent to stay with my aunt or grandparents. When I was six things were so bad that I was sent to stay with my aunt in Northumberland for an entire term, which I spent at a primary school in Morpeth. My classmates clearly thought of me as an effete southerner and I was bullied from time to time.

Whether my father's illness was genetic or caused by his upbringing I know not. I suspect the latter as neither my brother nor I have been afflicted. He certainly can't have been helped by his relationship with his mother, who once, in my presence, turned to him and said, 'Oh Leonard, it's such a pity it was Brian who was killed in the war rather than you.' His younger brother Brian had been killed as a Fleet Air Arm pilot in the invasion of Salerno.

Of course, the main burden was borne by my mother. Apart from having to cope with the turbulent mood swings, she spent her life being terrified that he would lose his job as a Taxing Master and we would face financial ruin. Tragically, it became too much for her and she killed herself in 1967 at the age of fifty-five. I was twenty-four and my brother only twelve.

My father never did lose his job, retired at the age of sixty-nine and died in 1998 at the age of eighty-six. Responsibility for his health devolved primarily on me after my mother died.

Inevitably, with elderly people the line between mental illness and eccentricity is a narrow one. Was it eccentricity that made my father direct every woman who came into the bookshop he ran in Barnes after his retirement to the 'sexually explicit love poems'? Was it eccentricity when, in front of my children at lunch, on being asked whether he had ever eaten snails, he replied that he never had nor had he ever had sex with a black girl? Was it eccentricity when he could not be prevented from leaving the lunch table in the dining room of the National Liberal Club and urinating in the fireplace in the library, as the Gents was too far away? Eccentricity was certainly no defence in the view of the club's committee, who eventually asked him to resign his membership of over fifty years. This put a new perspective on F. E. Smith's famous remark in 1922. The Tory politician and lawyer had been accustomed to stop off at the National Liberal Club to use the Gents on his walk from the Temple to the House of Commons after lunch. When the Tories pulled out of the coalition government, the club committee instructed the hall porter to deny Smith access. When stopped, Smith is alleged to have looked round the marble walls and commented, 'Good God! You mean it's a club as well?' Funny from F. E. Smith, but my father had no such witticism and resignation was unavoidable.

My mother had always refused to have my father sectioned, taking the view I think that this would be a step too far for his employers. I did not have any such compunction as, particularly during manic episodes, he needed immediate medical treatment. I suspect that during a manic episode bipolar individuals think that they are the only sane person, so are unlikely to agree to voluntary admission to hospital. That was certainly the case with my father.

I had to have him sectioned on two occasions, on the second narrowly escaping a disaster. When an individual is sectioned he or she has the right to appeal to a judge, who comes to the hospital to hear the application. This is obviously a protection to enable individuals subject to abuse of power by relatives to obtain their freedom. My father, by then in his late seventies, exercised his right to appeal and the judge duly arrived for the hearing in the hospital in Epsom, Surrey.

I was unable to attend but my brother, by then a Church of England vicar, could do so. When asked by the judge why I, a London solicitor, and my brother, a respected vicar, had made submissions that our father should be detained for medical assistance, apparently he gave a plausible, articulate response that we had just got it wrong. According to my brother, all was going badly until right at the end. Our father had privately published a short autobiography called *Law, Love and Laughter*. He advanced on the judge waving a dog-eared book and offering to provide a signed copy. The judge at that moment realised the problem.

But treatment improved and modern drugs could even out the mood swings, although they did nothing for the eccentricity. Whether sympathy and understanding of mental illness has grown in parallel with improvements in treatment, I doubt. Norman Lamb, the Liberal

Democrat health minister in the coalition government, certainly accepts that this is a problem and is correctly pressing for mental illness to be given equal priority with physical conditions. He has some way to go.

—CHAPTER FOUR—

THE USA

F OR MY GENERATION at Oxford, the United States was an integral part of our lives. We realised that without American assistance the Second World War would have been lost. The killing of President Kennedy in Dallas was an event that confirmed our solidarity with our American cousins.

So the opportunity to visit the United States was too good to miss. By the time I left Oxford I had arranged my solicitor's articles with the Lincoln's Inn firm Frere Cholmeley. But before joining them I was offered a year's teaching post at Northwestern University in Chicago.

In the 1960s, a number of American law schools offered

junior teaching positions to English graduates. This was primarily because law is a postgraduate degree in the United States and after their undergraduate and graduate degrees young Americans wanted to qualify for the Bar rather than teach basic law courses, even if subsequently they returned to academic life. After I came back to the United Kingdom this all changed with the escalation of the Vietnam War. Teachers could obtain an exemption from the draft so there was no further need to recruit teachers from overseas.

President Johnson was significantly increasing America's involvement in Vietnam while at the same time attempting to broker a peace settlement. The war had little impact on the university or me, except for an incident when I gave a poor mark to a student for an essay he submitted to me. When he asked to see me he urged me to alter his mark, otherwise he would have to leave the university, be sent to Vietnam and his death would be on my conscience. I thought he was bluffing and refused to change his mark. I was right and he was still a student when I returned to England.

The Chicago climate had two extremes in the year I was there – an ice-cold winter exacerbated by the perpetual wind, and a searingly hot summer, with only a brief spring and autumn.

Although Northwestern University is based in the

Chicago suburb of Evanston, the law school is in downtown Chicago, close to the lake. So I had a wonderful year in that fascinating city. My teaching requirements were fairly basic, but the real excitement was exposure to the faculty. A number were involved in politics for either the Republicans or the Democrats. Chicago itself was a hive of political activity and was run by Richard Daley, who is now generally accepted to have rigged the 1960 election to deliver Illinois to Jack Kennedy, without which Kennedy would have lost and Richard Nixon won. Joseph Kennedy, the candidate's father, had paid substantial sums in bribes and had paid the mafia to deliver the votes in Chicago. Before he was killed in 1963 President Kennedy was apparently asked by a close friend why, if his father was buying the election in Illinois, it was so close, and he retorted that his father would never have paid for a landslide.

Jim Thompson was a young, good-looking criminal law teacher. He first drew national attention when, as federal prosecutor in Illinois, he obtained a corruption conviction against leading aides of Major Daley. On the back of that success he was elected as the Republican governor of Illinois, a position he held for fourteen years, the longest in Illinois history. Another political luminary on the Democrat side was Dawn Netsch, who died in 2013 aged eighty-six. Dawn had been actively involved in Adlai Stevenson's unsuccessful campaign for the presidency in 1952 against Dwight D. Eisenhower. She subsequently had an active political career, being surprisingly elected as the Illinois state comptroller and then unsuccessfully running as the Democrat candidate for governor of Illinois.

But the faculty did not consist only of aspiring politicians. At the other academic extreme was Professor Alexander Nekam, who by then was the country's specialist in the comparison between Western legal systems and the customary law practised by African tribes, particularly Ugandan. Alex Nekam was Hungarian and came to the United States as a refugee from Communism. His early life was spent in the Hungarian civil service and he had witnessed first-hand the corrupt overthrow by the Communists by 1949 of the non-Communist government elected after Germany's defeat in 1945. In light of my subsequent experience in Russia, one anecdote from him strikes a chord. In either 1947 or 1948 Alexander was part of the Hungarian delegation to Moscow to discuss bilateral relations with Russia. In effect, the discussions were held in order to receive Stalin's instructions for the Communist takeover of Hungary. What amused Alexander was that every two or three hours, after aggressive bullying of the Hungarians, the Russian chairman banged the table and said it was time for thirty minutes' compulsory fraternisation – so they all went outside to the garden and discussed

culture, history and their families before returning to the
meeting room for a further period of bullying.

My closest relationship on the faculty was with Jack
Heinz, to whom I reported and who became a great friend.
Jack's expertise was in the study of lawyers and law firms,
using sociological methods to distinguish differences in
the organisation and delivery of legal services and the relationships among varying types of lawyers. For forty years
after I left Chicago he was on the faculty of Northwestern Law School and for a period was the director of the
American Bar Foundation.

But that was in the future. As a 22-year-old I found Jack
hugely glamorous. After graduating from Yale Law School,
Jack had just completed his military service as some sort of
social aide in Lyndon Johnson's White House, where his
responsibility seemed to have been to ensure that guests
had a good time. Apart from a lifetime of friendship, Jack
taught me two things that have stayed with me.

First, a love of wine. In 1965, despite the growth of California vineyards, wine was not widely drunk socially in
the United States. Indeed, if invited to a friend's house for
dinner the normal drink was either whisky – bourbon or
Scotch – or American martini – virtually neat gin. Indeed,
on one occasion when an American friend came to dinner, asked for a martini and was told we had no vermouth,
he said neat gin with ice would do. Sometimes I used to

wonder if this was to anaesthetise the palate from inedible food. But Jack was the exception. I had little experience of wine until I met him. In England I drank beer, having overindulged in sherry and port at university. Jack taught me to enjoy wine from Europe and the United States and is responsible for my lifetime love, sometimes to excess, but always with pleasure.

Second, a profound aversion to capital punishment. Jack had taken on pro bono the representation of Orville Waldron. Orville had been convicted of murder following a bar-room brawl while on parole for a second-degree murder conviction in Florida. Orville had been sentenced to death and was on death row in Joliet Prison near Chicago, where I had to visit him to obtain his signature on some papers that Jack needed for an appeal. I am still haunted by the memory of the visit and particularly his last words as I left: 'I really hope you can do something for me, Mr Razzall.' Some understatement.

I left Chicago long before Orville Waldron's appeals were exhausted and I suspect he was the beneficiary of the US Supreme Court's decision that the Illinois statute, which had formed the basis of his death sentence, was unconstitutional. The legal arguments against capital punishment have varied before the Supreme Court over the years, but the death penalty itself has never been found to be unconstitutional. But from the day I met Orville

Waldron I recognised that capital punishment should have
no place in civilised society.

Jan Waltz was a flamboyant teacher of tort law. During
my time he wrote a book on the trial of Jack Ruby. Ruby
had shot and killed Lee Harvey Oswald, the assassin of
President Kennedy, with the result that Oswald could not
be put on trial.

The Kennedy killing had occurred two years previously and had seared my generation, as Kennedy had
seemed to epitomise the bright future rather than the grey
past. I had lapped up stories of the Kennedy White House,
soon called 'Camelot' by the press, and loved the anecdote
about the first glamorous soirée held by the new President.
To signify the break with the dullness of the Eisenhower
years, a party was arranged at which the guests were the
cream of American artistic society – musicians, painters,
writers. Allegedly, in welcoming the guests, the President
opined that it was the greatest collection of talent gathered
in that room in the White House since Thomas Jefferson
had dined there alone.

We all remember where we were when President Kennedy was shot. I had come out of dinner in the college hall
to find my American friends sobbing in the quad. I then
became fascinated with the different theories surrounding
the assassination and have continued to be so. The inquiry
by Chief Justice Warren found that Lee Harvey Oswald

acted alone. The first alternative theory was that it was orchestrated by the Cubans, in revenge for the Bay of Pigs fiasco and the attempts by the CIA to murder Fidel Castro. This view was supported by evidence of the increase in radio traffic from Havana to Cuban agents in Florida on the day in question.

The second theory, which seemed more plausible and which I still believe, was that it was the mafia. The President's father had paid the mafia to deliver Illinois for his son in the election, apparently on the basis that the new administration would go easy on mafia activities. Robert Kennedy, the President's brother and the Attorney General, was reneging on this deal.

The most bizarre theory was explained to me recently by James Reston Jr, who coincidentally had worked on David Frost's iconic television interview with President Nixon. His thesis, as reflected in his book *The Accidental Victim*, is that Oswald's proposed victim was not President Kennedy at all, but the then Governor of Texas, John Connolly. According to James Reston, Oswald had been dishonourably discharged from the US Navy and he blamed John Connolly for failing to reinstate him when the latter was Navy Secretary. There seemed to me to be a fatal flaw in James Reston's thesis. The first shot by Oswald touched the President's neck and hit John Connolly, who was sitting in the back of the car, very hard and he collapsed on his wife's lap, putting him out of sight of the gunman. If Connolly was the target, why did Oswald shoot again with the shot that killed the President? When I put this to James Reston, his response was that a psychiatrist had told him that when a gunman fires once he finds it difficult not to fire again!

I am afraid I prefer the mafia theory.

My closest friend at law school was René Joliet. He was a Belgian from Liège, where his father ran Piedboeuf, the large Belgian brewer. Suave and volatile, René epitomised the English image of the Gaul. René was in Chicago to study the relationship between European and American antitrust law and particularly whether the US doctrine of the Rule of Reason had any equivalence in Articles 85 and 86 of the Treaty of Rome. I gave him some help, but our main contact was in the bars near the law school where we put the world to rights. Until I met René I had not appreciated the hostility between the French-speaking and Flemish-speaking Belgians. For a rational man, René's views were extraordinary. His rant against the Flemish made the Protestant/Catholic divide in Northern Ireland look positively peaceful.

René went on to great things – professor of law at Liège University and then a judge on the European Court of Justice until his sad death at the age of fifty-eight.

We had several holidays in Europe together, the most

memorable being in Czechoslovakia in 1968. This started strangely, when I received a visit from a Foreign Office official who asked me to carry a letter to the former girlfriend of a friend of mine, whom they realised I would see when I was in Prague. How they knew and what was in the letter I was not told. After a number of days in Bohemia we arrived in Prague and I delivered the letter. The tension in the city was palpable. The Russians had invaded and overthrown the Dubček government, thereby killing off hopes for a thaw in the regime. There was to be a huge student demonstration in the main square and René and I decided to go and observe. We were standing at the back of the square when Russian tanks started firing over the heads of the demonstrators. We looked at each other, bolted for the car and drove straight to the Austrian border. Many years later in Prague I could see the bullet holes on the walls above where we had been standing.

I had a taste of René's Gallic volatility when we arrived in Vienna and, after an argument, he punched me on the jaw and knocked me to the ground. But our friendship was not damaged.

When I first arrived in the United States I naively believed that not only was London the centre of the English-speaking world, but that Americans would understand that. I soon realised how wrong I was.

I am not quite sure what the Americans I met made

of me. I certainly quickly appreciated that we were two countries divided by a common language.

The best example occurred many years later at Los Angeles Airport. I was attending the Democrat convention in Pasadena and a car had been arranged to pick me up. When no car appeared for 'Razzall' or 'Tim Razzall', I suggested to the dispatcher that the booking might have been for 'Lord Razzall'. 'Lord, Lord, what sort of a first name is that?' was his reply.

But cultural differences emerged from the start.

I suspect the nadir of my experience there came in Lake Forest one winter evening. Lake Forest is a suburb of Chicago, at that time the home of many wealthy white business people. The university had created a programme in which non-Americans were allocated to a family charged with looking after us if we needed help. I had been allocated to a couple in Lake Forest and was invited to dinner. I arrived at a palatial property – I doubt if I had ever been in such a large private house – and was welcomed with the usual pre-dinner drinks.

There was another couple there, to whom I was introduced but with whom I had no pre-dinner conversation. When we sat down, the male guest started to lead us in prayer. I had never experienced this before and assumed it was the type of joke John Cleese later made famous, of the 'what a way to spend Easter' variety, and, emboldened by the half pint of gin I had consumed, made some witty crack. Nobody laughed and it emerged that this was the local Episcopalian minister. I was not invited there again.

My experiences of the United States have been pretty extensive. I was lucky to be invited to the Democrat conventions in Los Angeles in 2000 and Boston in 2004, where I realised how all-pervasive the need for the right television image had become. I saw the beginning of the now ubiquitous attempts to drill down to and understand the likely reaction and voting propensity of every voter through the developing use of the internet. In 2004 I was stunned by the rhetoric of a newly elected black senator from Chicago who gave a keynote speech. My colleague and I agreed that he would go far.

I had already met Bill Clinton, or rather shaken him by the hand, at the Hay-on-Wye book festival in 2001. Revel Guest, very much the creator of the festival, had arranged drinks at her house before dinner so that a number of us could meet the great man. He arrived late – typically, I understand – and we all stood around drinking on the lawn in the evening sun. His helicopter eventually arrived and we lined up to shake his hand. When it was my turn he greeted me with, 'Good evening, sir.'

'There's no need to rub it in that I'm older than you,' I replied. He laughed.

Dinner was in a tent at the festival with I suppose

a hundred or so guests. When we sat down I was two down from the President, with Gail Rebuck, the publisher, between us. Needless to say, Gail Rebuck preferred to talk to the guest of honour. Opposite me was Louis de Bernières, author of *Captain Corelli's Mandolin*, with whom I had an entertaining conversation. Next to him was Germaine Greer, who took no interest in us but, as the evening wore on, was becoming more and more frustrated as she could not get into the conversation with the President. I suggested that she should remind him of the occasion when she came to give a talk to University College Oxford students about her book *The Female Eunuch* and a young Bill Clinton sitting at the back put his hand up and asked whether a poor boy from Arkansas would do. 'Who the fuck told you that?' she raged, got up, left the table and never came back. I had read the story in *Vanity Fair*.

My last exposure to President Clinton occurred some years later. The hedge fund industry has an annual dinner to raise money for charity. I was invited one year to Marlborough House in Pall Mall. I remember that there were twelve or so auction prizes, none of which went for less than a million pounds. Walking into the courtyard of Marlborough House, guests were surprised to be serenaded by seventy-five saxophonists. The reason was that Bill Clinton was attending, as part of the proceeds were going to his

Africa charity and he had memorably played the saxophone on American television. Again, he arrived about an hour and a half late, accompanied by a large security detail. I have no idea whether the seventy-five saxophonists played until his arrival. Sadly, there was no Germaine Greer to enliven proceedings. Our paths have not crossed since.

I cannot visit Manhattan without remembering the events at a huge auction sale by Parke-Bernet of French impressionist paintings that could have killed my legal career at birth. I had just started as a solicitor at Frere Cholmeley and was in Manhattan on client business. Philip Kaplan, a partner in the New York law firm I was dealing with, had been handling the legal details of the auction and kindly invited me to accompany his wife, Siggi. He would be backstage. When the auction started I realised that Siggi had a list of reserve prices and I thought it would be fun to participate without fear so long as I stayed below the reserve. So I loved bidding $15 million for a Monet painting with a reserve of $20 million.

When I told Philip Kaplan over dinner later what a thrill it had been to put my hand up with a $15 million bid without risk of acceptance Philip went white and explained that all of the reserve prices had been altered since he had given Siggi the list! I was never clear what would have happened if my bid had been accepted. I certainly did not have $15 million.

Even in the mid-1960s, politics in the United States was starting to polarise, although not to the extent that it did in later years, with the influence of the evangelical right and the Tea Party over the Republican Party. An early example of this polarisation was experienced by me in the late 1970s in California. My host in the wine country took me to dinner at the home of Tom Jordan, an oil and gas multimillionaire from Colorado who was creating Jordan's Winery, later famed for its Cabernet Sauvignon. The house was an integral part of the winery, designed to entertain major customers, which I certainly was not. After drinks we sat down for dinner, with me sitting next to Tom Jordan. Conversation was going well until he asked me whether I had any political views. When I told him that I was active in the Liberal Party, he turned to my host, told him that he did not allow liberals in his home and asked us to leave. I was later told that he had been an active member of the John Birch Society, an organisation that made our National Front look positively socialist.

But despite the false start in Lake Forest and my treatment by Tom Jordan, I fell in love with the country and have spent many happy times there in my life. My relationship with the United States has deepened as my son now lives in Los Angeles with his American wife.

—CHAPTER FIVE—

CRICKET

B EFORE I MOVE on to my professional and political life, this is perhaps the moment to describe the important role cricket has played.

I was introduced to cricket by my maternal grandfather, Pearson Knowles. He taught me to play with hours of patience in his garden in Colchester and from the age of six onwards I was a regular spectator either at Scarborough during the summer holidays or at the Oval. I remember my first county game well – Yorkshire against Warwickshire in 1949. I do not remember the scores but I do remember my mother's intolerance of the cricket bore on our left. After an hour in which he had never drawn breath during his demonstration of his encyclopaedic knowledge of the game, my mother turned to him, gestured at the umpire and asked him when the little man in the white coat would be given a go.

I can still see my grandfather when I was eight or nine sitting in an empty, rain-swept stand with his umbrella up. Play at the Scarborough cricket festival had been abandoned for the day and I was hanging about the dressing room door waiting to secure autographs.

My personal ambitions as a cricketer started early. I bowled at Len Hutton when I was ten years old. As the first professional to captain England, he was fresh from his triumph in winning the Ashes, much to the surprise of most of cricket's establishment, who believed that a professional would not be up to it.

Harrods had hired him and Denis Compton to perform an indoor net in their Knightsbridge store at Christmas. For sixpence any boy could bowl an over at the great men. Of course Denis Compton let any young boy have his wicket, but Len Hutton played as if we were Lindwall or Miller.

Being a boy of Yorkshire origins myself, Len remained my hero. As a young man he had broken the world record with his 364 at the Oval in 1938. His arm injury during the war restricted his mobility with the bat, but he remained England's premier batsman until his retirement in the late 1950s, with a cover drive to die for, as Harold Pinter has immortalised.

I batted with him once after he retired. At least I got to the crease when he was at the other end. It was an MCC game against my old school, St Paul's. They made about 120 and Len opened the batting in our innings. I was scheduled to bat number 4 and as he ground his way to a slow 50 I feared I would not get to the wicket. On 120, with the scores level, a wicket fell and I went out to the non-strikers' end. Len pushed a single and the match was over without me facing a ball. So I can say I batted with the great Len Hutton.

We all repaired to a local pub in the Hammersmith Road opposite Olympia and much beer was consumed. It was the same pub that had been a teenage haunt out of the range of our school masters. After a while, Len engaged me in a serious conversation about 'young people today'.

I was twenty at the time. It was clear he was talking about his sons. He told me that he had sent them off to public school but really didn't understand them any more and felt he had lost any relationship with them. I realised that notwithstanding his gigantic achievements he still felt isolated and alienated by 'the establishment', who had not wanted him to captain England. It was a class thing.

At closing time we stumbled out into the road and we both urinated in a nearby gutter. I never saw him again but he remains my hero to this day.

I suppose I was a pretty good schoolboy cricketer. By

fourteen, I was already nearly six foot, so on Sundays could play with the men at my father's club in Acton. My father played every weekend until his early fifties and was probably the worst player ever to have played club cricket for so long. He couldn't throw overarm, couldn't bowl and, at the crease, had only one stroke. He would put his left leg firmly down the pitch and attempt to hit the ball to square leg. It was no surprise that a well-pitched-up delivery would dismiss him every time. Yet such is the allure of the game that he came back for more every weekend in the summer.

I played in the First XI at school for a number of years and in my last year was selected to play at Lord's for the Southern Schools against the Rest. Although it was a two-day fixture I never went on the field as we had two days of torrential rain. But I do remember the awe I felt when entering the iconic pavilion that had been built in the nineteenth century and which still reeks of the history of the game.

At school I first came across a number of giants of the past who still turned out for the wandering club sides on our fixture list. For several years the MCC side against us was run by the legendary C. B. Clarke, known to all as Bertie. Bertie had played as a nineteen-year-old in the West Indies team that toured England in 1939, just before the outbreak of war. He then qualified as a doctor but played

first-class cricket again in the 1950s, I think for Essex.
Bertie was undoubtedly the best leg spinner that I, and
I suspect most others, had ever faced. He had everything.
A prodigious leg break, a top spinner and, most alarmingly,
two googlies, one you could read and another you could
not. Bertie stopped bringing the MCC team to St Paul's
as he was sent to prison for performing illegal abortions.
But he re-emerged later in my life when I was playing club
cricket and for some reason he was captain of the BBC.

A highlight in my last year at school in 1962 was to face
an MCC team with Alec Bedser as the opening bowler.
For ten years after the Second World War Alec Bedser had
carried the England opening attack, dismissed the great
Don Bradman on several occasions and had a face recognised throughout the cricket world. He had just retired
from the first-class game. But nevertheless as he marked
out his run he must have been startled by the umpire's
gentle request, 'Are you bowling right arm over, sir?'
I faced the great man for a number of overs. Although he
had lost the pace from his pomp, his skill with the ball was
extraordinary. His stock ball was a booming inswinger but
every five or six balls the inswinger would pitch on the leg
stump and move to the off – a perfect leg cutter with no
apparent change of action.

Alec went on to chair the England selectors and took
an unsuccessful England team to Australia. Years later

I would meet him several times as a guest in the Surrey committee room at the Oval. He was interested in me as he and his twin brother had started life as solicitors' clerks before becoming professional cricketers. By this time he was lugubrious and pessimistic in the extreme. He did not understand the modern game. He could not fathom why fast bowlers kept being injured. His generation had bowled thousands of overs a year without injury. To him, the modern player was no longer obsessed by cricket as his generation had been and was therefore not as good. It was sad to listen to.

At school I also met for the first time the legendary Oliver Battcock. Oliver had started as an actor in the 1930s, but took every summer off to play cricket. Wisden will tell of his exploits in club cricket and for Buckinghamshire in the Minor Counties competition. He had started as a fast medium bowler and left-handed middle-order batsman. By the time I first faced him he had slowed down with age, but still possessed a sharp outswing and a prodigious off cutter. For over thirty years he had played cricket all summer and spent the winter at the playhouse in Salisbury where, as Oliver Gordon, he was a star in the annual Christmas pantomime.

After I left school I played a number of games for Oliver in club cricket. Memories of Oliver echo the Neville Cardus phrase 'the burnt-out Junes revive'. I remember his kindness and generosity when, as an eighteen-year-old, I was having dinner after a game in a team of adults who had jobs. Oliver gave me some cash with the explanation that the club always subsidised students on these occasions. Years later, of course, I realised that this had come from his own pocket.

I remember the deep embarrassment at fielding on the boundary in a big game against the military at Aldershot and dropping three catches off three consecutive balls off Oliver's bowling. I can't remember whether he laughed more than me.

But mostly I remember how he linked us all to the golden age of cricket through the length of his career. He told me once that in the 1930s he had been playing for Buckinghamshire and was due to bat at number 7. As the opening batsman walked to the wicket, his captain enquired why he was not padded up. 'I'm number 7,' he replied. 'Exactly,' said his captain. 'Can't you see S. F. Barnes is opening the bowling?' S. F. Barnes was probably England's greatest bowler before and after the First World War. To plagiarise Scott Fitzgerald, with Oliver we beat back against the current, borne back ceaselessly to the past.

When I started playing adult cricket, the Second World War had started only twenty years previously and I was playing with or against veterans of that conflict. Jimmy Grey was a case in point. At the age of eighteen I shared a room with him on tour and late one night after an alcoholic evening he reminisced about his experiences in the Battle of Britain. He told me that after surviving that period, life had been an anticlimax. Even at my young age I think I grasped what he meant. What I certainly did not understand was his description of the game of ashtray tennis they played in the officers' mess on their return from a flight operation.

Apparently they divided the room into two teams, with each man armed with a heavy cut-glass ashtray. The two teams lined up opposite each other, turned the lights off and served in turn across the room in total darkness. He had no recollection of the casualties. I do remember that facing the fast bowler the next day instilled less fear than I would have felt facing a cut-glass ashtray in the dark.

After school my first two summers at Oxford were dominated by cricket. A good first summer for the Oxford Authentics, the university second team, was followed by a season for the Blues team, although I was not selected for the game against Cambridge so missed out on a 'Blue'. In those days the university team involved three-day first-class games against the counties or leading clubs, which were classified as first class. My first game was against a Free Foresters side full of first-class cricketers, including the legendary Frank Worrell. As a huge fan of C. L. R. James's seminal work *Beyond a Boundary*, I was stunned to find myself on the same pitch as Frank Worrell. In his book, James equates the fight against racial prejudice in the emerging West Indies with the struggle to have a black captain of the West Indies cricket team, which had often played with a white captain and ten black players. With Worrell's appointment, West Indies cricket flourished. In 1960 he had captained the West Indies in Australia, where the famous tie occurred in the Brisbane test. He had retired from Test cricket at the end of the previous year's series in England. So I felt I was playing against a living legend. I can see him now, sitting in the Kings Arms pub in Oxford at the end of first day's play, regaling us with stories of his career. His grace and modesty demonstrated why C. L. R. James had been right to choose him as the standard bearer for the fight for racial equality. He epito-mised the aphorism 'what do they know of cricket who only cricket know'. His death from leukaemia only a few years later was a tragedy.

My first game against a county side was against Essex. We batted first and when I went in I was facing Robin Hobbs, the England leg spinner. After I had taken guard and Hobbs was in his run-up I heard the wicket keeper behind me say to the short leg, 'Eh, John, do you think that's his prick or his thigh pad?' Other county games fol-lowed against Sussex, Hampshire and Gloucestershire. John Martin and I bowled out Derbyshire for just over

a hundred and we would probably have won had it not
been for the intervention of rain. I was twelfth man against
Worcestershire and fielded for most of the game due to
an injury to one of our players. Basil D'Oliveira had been
brought over from apartheid South Africa by John Arlott
to make his way in first-class cricket, barred to him in
South Africa. He was not yet qualified to play in the county
championship but could play in other first-class games. He
made a century against us and I remember the power of
his stroke play, particularly off the back foot with virtually
no backlift. He went on to great success for Worcestershire and England, but I suppose his greatest success
in the history of cricket was to be indirectly responsible for
the suspension of South Africa from Test cricket in 1970.

England was due to tour South Africa in that year and
when the tour team was announced Basil D'Oliveira was
omitted, despite his century in the last Test of the previous
summer. In those days, England tours were officially MCC
tours and I attended the MCC members' meeting where
a motion to cancel the tour was to be debated. In those
days the attitude that sport should not intervene in politics
was prevalent, particularly in right-wing circles. Despite
passionate argument against the tour by John Arlott and
Michael Brearley and despite the suspicion that the South
African government had threatened privately to cancel the
tour if Basil D'Oliveira was selected, the members voted

by a majority not to cancel the tour. There was no doubt
which way I voted. Alec Douglas-Home, only a few years
after taking over from Harold Macmillan as Prime Minister
and losing to Harold Wilson in the 1964 general election,
took the establishment line that provoking South Africa
would be a mistake and the MCC establishment followed
Alec. In the event, when Tom Cartwright dropped out of
the tour through injury the selectors were forced to pick
Basil and the tour was cancelled.

But all that was in the future. I can still see Basil at the
end of each day's play standing in the door of our dressing room, having changed out of his whites, hoovering up
the conversation of young students whose paths he could
not cross in South Africa as we were white.

People have asked me who I felt was the best county
batsman I bowled at that season. I have no doubt it was
Roy Marshall, who was playing for Hampshire. Roy had
played Test cricket for the West Indies, so although he
had settled in England he was not eligible for the England
team. I bowled probably my best spell ever against him
and almost dismissed him when the ball fell just short of
midwicket. Would my cricket career have been different
if the catch had been held? Who knows?

But the best batsman I bowled at that season was not
playing county cricket. The South African schools were
on tour and had a fixture in Oxford. I bowled against a

smallish young man who, in my first over, hit six good length balls for four. It had never happened to me before or since.

When we came off I asked the South African manager who the boy was. 'Oh, that's Barry Richards,' he said. 'We think he's going to be rather good.' My bruised ego recovered when I hooked their fast bowler for six. I discovered later that he was Mike Procter. Richards and Procter went on to great things.

After my second year at Oxford I realised that the first-class game was not for me. I had narrowly failed to win the coveted 'Blue' and although both Middlesex and Hampshire showed some interest in my services I decided that my life was not destined to follow the path of serious cricket. I was just not good enough to achieve at the highest level.

But that did not mean I abandoned cricket. I had a glorious twenty years playing serious league cricket at weekends – a welcome contrast to my life in the law and politics. The details of games long past escape me, but the memories of those I played with and against remain.

In my early twenties I took a team to play Brondesbury, who were captained by Michael Cockerell. Michael went on to make political programmes for the BBC, so our paths crossed again many years later. I asked Michael what sort of a team he had. 'Not bad and we have a fifteen-year-old who we think is going to be pretty good.' He was right. The fifteen-year-old Mike Gatting made seventy-odd against us and went on to captain Middlesex and England.

I sat next to Mike Gatting at a lunch years later, and he remembered his time as a boy at Brondesbury with affection. Our conversation reminded me of the old barrister's maxim never to ask a witness a question if you were not sure how they would answer. Nigel Farage, the leader of UKIP, was sitting opposite us and I complained to him that Malcolm Pearson, his predecessor as UKIP leader, turned every topic in a House of Lords debate into a European issue, however far-fetched. 'Come on, Tim,' he replied, 'you know every issue relates to Europe.' I turned to Mike Gatting for support.

'Clearly cricket has no European dimension.'

'You are wrong there,' he responded. 'County cricket is being ruined by Europe.'

'How come?'

'Because Brussels employment law means that Australians with Italian ancestry can come and play here so there are fewer opportunities for our young players.'

'I told you so, Tim,' said Nigel Farage, with an enormous grin. I had learnt my lesson.

Cricket is a game that seems to attract eccentrics. But I never met a cricketer more eccentric than Stuart Feldman, who must be the least athletic sportsman I ever played with.

Stuart bowled slow leg breaks and googlies – very slow – with an action that defies explanation. As he approached the bowling crease off five or six paces, both arms went forward in the style of a butterfly swimmer and the ball was released from his right hand, almost as an afterthought. It was as if Piggy from *Lord of the Flies* had metamorphosed into a praying mantis, or Conan Doyle's Spedegue's Dropper had come alive from his dream. His fielding was indescribably bad. Always at mid-on, he could usually stop a ball hit straight at him, but anything he had to chase invariably turned a single into three. To watch him pursue the ball was to watch an octopus struggling on dry land.

But what a bowler! In the 1950s he played for Hornsey on the north London circuit and terrorised the opposition. The ball came very slowly through the air, dipped onto a length and turned sharply either way. Countless batsmen were deceived by the flight and were stumped or bowled or caught in a slog to deep midwicket. Hauls of seven, eight or nine wickets were commonplace.

In his professional life he was a practicing solicitor with a sharp brain. For a long time he was a director of Hendon Town, the amateur football club, until he resigned on account of the sham amateurism that prevailed in those days, as he later told me. Illicit payments were made to players, who were in reality professionals.

I met him when he re-joined the Old Paulines in the

1960s and had several happy years with him. With the advent of league cricket, let alone his advancing years, Stuart's playing days were numbered. His fielding leaked too many runs. My last memory epitomises this wise, gentle man. He had never taken all ten wickets in an innings. We were playing at our home ground and Stuart had taken the first nine. Number 11 struck the ball high in the air in the midwicket area, where two of our fielders converged in an attempt to catch the ball. A terrible collision occurred as the fielders clashed heads and the ball fell to the ground. Blood gushed from one of the fielder's heads in huge dollops. As the stretcher came onto the field, Stuart went pale and almost fainted. He couldn't bear the sight of blood so couldn't carry on. So he never got his ten wickets.

He died in the 1970s far too young.

Cricket has also attracted countless luminaries of the literary and journalistic worlds, from Conan Doyle through J. M. Barrie to Harold Pinter. But I doubt if there has been a more enthusiastic aficionado than Michael Parkinson. Readers of his autobiography will know of his opening the batting for Barnsley with Dickie Bird and of his later achievements with Maidenhead and Bray.

I met Michael when we were both guest speakers at a Datchet Cricket Club annual dinner. I forget the content of his speech but I will never forget his behaviour. Most television stars, as by then he was, arrive just before dinner, sit at the top table, make their speech and, after a few perfunctory thank yous, leave, claiming they have to be up early. Not Michael Parkinson. He and I were the last to leave and after dinner he had talked with interest to anyone who wanted to ask him questions from the serious to the most banal. What a star, I thought.

Cricket has pervaded all my life. How the game has crossed different aspects of my career was demonstrated by my later friendship with the former England captain Colin Cowdrey. Colin was nominated as a life peer by John Major, a lifelong cricket fan. We became friends and spent many a happy hour over a drink in the House of Lords bar while waiting to vote. Colin was full of anecdotes. He was tickled by the occasion he sponsored David Sheppard, who was made a life peer by Tony Blair following his retirement as Bishop of Liverpool. The other sponsor was Robert Runcie, the former Archbishop of Canterbury. As they removed their robes after the ceremony, Robert Runcie told David Sheppard that he assumed he would be sitting as a cross-bencher. When told by David Sheppard that he was taking the Labour whip he turned to Colin with the same assumption. When told that Colin took the Tory whip, he was shocked. 'How ecumenical!' was his response.

Mostly Colin and I talked cricket. One of his strangest recollections was his experience on his first overseas tour, to South Africa. Wally Hammond had been England's premier batsman from the late 1920s until his retirement shortly after the war. He had moved to Cape Town and Colin was invited to dinner at his palatial home. Demonstrating the strange behaviour that was probably a symptom of the syphilis which apparently killed him, he instructed his house boy to bring a box of hen's eggs out to the lawn. As Colin was a slip fielder, Wally proposed to instruct him on how to field there. He hurled egg after egg at Colin from close range with the admonition to keep his hands soft to avoid breaking the shells. That was the way he should catch the hard cricket ball.

Colin told me another story that he said demonstrated Wally Hammond's descent into mental illness. This had been passed on to Colin by Sam Cook, the Gloucestershire left arm spinner who played the odd game for England after the war.

Apparently, when the young Sam Cook went for a trial with Gloucestershire, Wally Hammond as captain took him into the nets to see how he could bowl. Instead of playing each ball with the face of the bat, he insisted on using only the edge. The ball was turning all over the place, but he hit every one. Either brilliant eccentricity or incipient mania!

Colin's death deprived me of wonderful evenings. I could help him with politics – he didn't really understand it – and he reaffirmed my love of cricket.

Rumour had it in cricketing circles that Colin had been a rather indecisive captain of the England cricket team. I was having a drink one evening with Peter Parfitt, the old Middlesex and England left-hand batsman, who described to me his experience of his first Test match for England. Colin Cowdrey was captain and had arranged to pick up Peter the day before the game and drive him up to Leeds, where the game started the next day. Peter described his astonishment as a new boy at how Colin cross-questioned him about who should bowl, from which end, in which order and what field should be placed. Peter did his best, but when they arrived at the pre-match dinner in Leeds, Freddie Trueman took over.

'Don't worry, skipper, I'll bowl from the Kirkstall Lane End; four slips, two gullies and two short legs and I get 7 for 27.'

On the same occasion I told Peter Parfitt about Denis Compton letting me bowl him out at Harrods all those years ago. He told me about the first time he met Denis Compton. He was a young man in his first season for Middlesex and in the first game he was twelfth man. Denis Compton had not appeared at pre-season nets, but Middlesex were batting first and Denis was down to bat at number four. Denis arrived just as the Middlesex openers were going out to bat. After enquiring who Peter Parfitt was, and establishing that he was twelfth man, he said that he seemed to have forgotten his bat and could he borrow Peter's. He went into bat, scored a hundred, and never missed a ball. No training, no nets, but what a genius, thought Peter.

Cricket is a game that seems to attract great interest in parliamentarians. The two keenest I have come across never played. William Rees-Mogg became editor of *The Times* and was a prolific journalist for the remainder of his life. His first claim to fame was recorded by Simon Raven in his autobiography. The star cricketers in the Charterhouse First XI were Simon, Jim Prior, who later became a Tory Cabinet minister, and young Peter May, who went on to captain England. William Rees-Mogg was the scorer, but remained a lifelong cricket fan.

Sir Alan Haselhurst, Tory Member of Parliament for Saffron Walden and deputy speaker of the House of Commons until 2010, is also a huge cricket fan, at one time sitting on the Essex county cricket committee, despite the fact that, like William Rees-Mogg, he was also only a scorer in his younger days.

There can be no greater cricket fan than Peter Brooke, now Lord Brooke of Sutton Mandeville. When he was chairman of the Tory Party in the John Major government he used to confuse political journalists by answering questions as to how the government were doing with the cricketing analogy of 91 for 4 wickets or 130 for 5. Cricket clearly runs in his family as his son Dan Brooke, a senior executive at Channel 4, is one of the few English bowlers to dismiss the great West Indian Gary Sobers. As Dan will wryly explain, it was the last ball of the over and the first five had gone for twenty-eight runs.

Some of my more memorable experiences as a player have come in my later years. My daughter Katie, by then a reporter on *Channel 4 News*, was in Sri Lanka on her honeymoon when the tsunami struck. She and her husband Oliver were safe and she was able to cover the aftermath of the disaster for her TV channel.

Later that year she and Oliver organised a charity cricket match to raise money for the village in Sri Lanka where they had stayed, which had been decimated by the disaster. I rather inveigled myself onto Oliver's team, ignoring Katie's warning that the opposition was rather good and that I might be a bit old.

I twisted Oliver's arm to put me on to bowl and, after a wicket fell, found myself bowling to Aravinda de Silva, who two years previously had been ranked as the best batsman in the world. I was bowling slow offspin and he took two to third man off the first two balls with reverse sweeps. The third ball of the over I threw up outside the leg stump and extraordinarily an arm ball hit his leg stump. The best wicket I had ever taken!

Lords and Commons cricket provides an opportunity

for players of all ages and in my latter years I have been able to take full advantage. A tour to Australia over New Year in 2007 coincided with a 5–0 victory for Australia in the Ashes series and defeat for us in our games against the Australian Parliament. But I was able to play at the Bowral in New South Wales, a ground dedicated to the great Don Bradman.

In 2010 I was invited to play in Corfu. The team was put together by Jonathan Marland, about to become the government minister in the House of Lords. Jonathan is a member of the exclusive club of ex-party treasurers, having raised money for the Tories under Michael Howard. The ground is in the middle of Corfu town and local Corfiots seemed oblivious to the dangers of a hard cricket ball as they walked with their children across the outfield, far too close to the play.

Cricket was introduced to Corfu in 1823 by the Royal Navy, which was stationed there as the United Kingdom had occupied Corfu at the end of the Napoleonic War. I was amused to discover the circumstances surrounding Corfu becoming part of Greece in the middle of the nineteenth century. Apparently Disraeli was the Tory Prime Minister and asked Gladstone if he would travel to Corfu to make recommendations about the island's future. It was as if David Cameron had asked Ed Miliband to sort out the Ukraine! In any event, Gladstone spent several months there and recommended an independent Corfu. The Corfiots opted for a union with Greece.

I had assumed that the opposition would be expats. Far from it – all eleven of our opponents were Corfiots. I discovered that there is a Greek league in which Corfu has four teams – so the game has been well entrenched since 1823.

With supreme political tact, Jonathan Marland engineered a tie by running himself out – the first tie in living memory on the ground.

In 2012 I was able to go to India to play the Indian Parliament. After two warm-up games we went to Dharamsala, home of the Dalai Lama, who apparently when in residence comes to the ground to bless the teams at the start of the game. With unfortunate timing, he was in London. At the dinner I discovered that Mohammad Azharuddin had become the Member of Parliament for the Moradabad constituency of Uttar Pradesh and was playing against us.

Mohammad had scored twenty-two centuries in Test cricket, including centuries in each of his first three Tests – never achieved before or since. Although a Muslim, he became a successful captain of the Indian team. Sadly, in 2000 he had been banned from cricket for life for match fixing.

I explained this the night before to our captain Matthew Hancock and drew his attention to the fact that

Mohammad's ban was from all cricket so we could have him banned from the game or we would be bound to lose. Matthew gently explained to me that as we were there to further relations with the Indian Parliament, this was probably not a good idea. I was right: Mohammad scored a century and we lost. Matthew was right: not only on diplomatic grounds, but also because, as we subsequently discovered, the Indian authorities had lifted the ban in 2006, much to the dismay of the world cricket authorities.

—CHAPTER SIX—

THE LAW

I N 1966 I came back from the United States to England to begin my articles at Frere Cholmeley in Lincoln's Inn Fields. In those days Frere Cholmeley was known primarily as an upmarket firm acting for the landed aristocracy and gentry. Inevitably, a significant number of partners were Old Etonians. As a young man with some conceit and self-confidence, I was amazed to be told by my father that Tom Dinwiddy, formerly a partner of the firm and now a colleague of his at the Law Courts, had stopped him in the street to enquire, 'How on earth did *your* boy get into my old firm?' I was not clear whether this was because I was not an Old Etonian or because he didn't like my father.

The firm had been founded in the mid-eighteenth century and 200 years of client documents were buried in the basement, known as muniments. We articled clerks had to perform a weekly stint in muniments, sorting and destroying files that were no longer required, to make more space. The basement was so deep you could hear the rumble of the Underground trains below. Frere Cholmeley of that period was epitomised by a letter I found written twenty years or so previously from a partner to a client, to the effect that there were only two things that mattered in life: 'Eton and the Guards'.

Work for the landed gentry or aristocracy certainly had its moments. Legend had it that after the Second World War a lawyer from the firm had been sent to Wiltshire to evict Cecil Beaton, the famous photographer, from the house he had occupied for years (subsequently owned by Madonna and Guy Ritchie). In those days it was common for the tenant of a large house to pay a peppercorn rent and take on full responsibility for maintenance. This was the case for Cecil Beaton, who had spent considerable sums maintaining and modernising the property.

On the death of the landlord, the firm's instructions were to obtain possession. When Cecil Beaton complained that his relationship with the landlord had always been good, that he had lovingly cared for the property and saw no reason to move, he was told that the instructions from the landlord's son were clear. He had to vacate the property as his wild parties were upsetting the pheasants.

By the time I arrived, a decision had been taken to develop a commercial practice, to which I was attached on qualifying and where I spent the next thirty years.

Inevitably, as a late entrant to the commercial world, with offices outside the city, Frere Cholmeley found it difficult to break into the world of city merchant banks and their clients. So some of the early corporate clients were on the racy side. When the Stock Exchange first introduced a ban on trading on inside information, I recall a client who expostulated that this would make it impossible for him to make any money.

I remember being sent to the Isle of Man to buy a racehorse for the billionaire John Kluge, at one time billed as the richest man in the United States. The owner of the horse was Robert Sangster, who was based on the Isle of Man but who owned Vernons Football Pools. So the first port of call was in Liverpool for a meeting at Vernons' headquarters. The contract was signed and I returned to London. Hardly a typical transaction had I been a traditional City lawyer!

As a postscript, I read later that John Kluge's then wife was in serious legal trouble for giving her guests machine gun-type weapons to shoot animals.

But other avenues beckoned and on qualification I

found myself assisting the partner representing John Lennon, George Harrison and Ringo Starr in a dispute with Paul McCartney.

The dispute arose following the death of the band's manager, Brian Epstein. Mick Jagger had recommended Allan Klein to John Lennon as Brian Epstein's successor, but Paul McCartney wanted to appoint his wife's father, John Eastman. As there was no formal partnership agreement, the legal issue was whether the decision to appoint the manager should be unanimous or subject to majority vote. The band had in fact stopped performing by then, probably at the instigation of George Harrison, who wanted to pursue a solo career, so the issue really turned on who should manage their money. We never discovered the answer to the legal issue as common sense prevailed and the case was settled. Thereafter, the firm went on to represent Apple Corps Limited, the holding company for the band's assets and income.

I have two clear recollections of John Lennon from that period. First, as the junior member of the team, being asked in 1971 to collect him from the reception area and bring him to the relevant meeting room. The reception area in 28 Lincoln's Inn Fields looked as if it had not changed since the 1920s. I was stunned to see John Lennon sitting next to the venerable Marquess of Salisbury, still a power in the Tory Party, and master of Hatfield House, the Elizabethan stately home. Their juxtaposition certainly demonstrated how the firm was changing. Whether they spoke to each other is not recorded.

Second, to discover, in the review of his finances, that he held £1 million in a current account with his bank. When asked by my colleague why he had so much on current account, he said that he felt he might always need ready money in an emergency! Although my involvement ceased as I was transferred to other duties, the Beatles were an integral part of the lives of anyone born after 1940 and were certainly part of mine.

My experience with the 'Fab Four' had in fact started earlier. In 1964, Jeffrey Archer, then at Brasenose College, Oxford, announced that Oxford students would raise a million pounds for Oxfam. A stiff task today, let alone in 1964. We went round with our collecting tins but that produced only petty cash.

Jeffrey's pièce de résistance was to induce the Beatles to visit Oxford to sponsor the appeal. He achieved this by contacting their manager Brian Epstein and reading him the headline the *Daily Mail* would run: 'Beatles refuse to back Oxfam appeal'.

A dinner was arranged at Vincent's Club, to which I was invited. The highlight for me was a visit to the urinal to find myself standing next to Ringo Starr and George Harrison.

'You'd better keep hold of that tight, George,' says Ringo.

'Why?' asks George.

'Well, if you're not careful that fucker Archer will chop if off and pickle it for Oxfam.'

I never found out how much money Jeffrey raised for Oxfam. But I had had my first Beatles experience.

This outburst by Ringo was clearly typical. I heard later that the critic Sheridan Morley asked Ringo what he thought of Jeffrey Archer.

'Not a bad chap,' he apparently replied. 'But he's the sort who would bottle my urine and sell it.'

A classic pattern for our rock music clients when they came to us was that after great success they felt they had been cheated in some way by their management. This was the case with Elton John, the Bee Gees and Deep Purple, the heavy metal rock band. I have no recollection of the nature of the dispute between the Deep Purple band members, which I dealt with, other than that it was settled at a lengthy meeting in New York where the warring managers were paid off to their satisfaction.

I do remember two events very clearly. The first occurred at lunch in Soho where I first met Deep Purple's John Lord and the drummer Ian Paice. It was an Italian restaurant, now no longer there, and after I'd introduced myself, Ian Paice asked me what I would like to eat. I asked him what he was going to have and he said, 'Mediterranean prawns and a veal chop.' I replied that I would have the same. When the waiter came to the table to take the order, Ian Paice asked for thirty-six Mediterranean prawns as a starter. Ian turned to me and when I replied that that was fine, he told me that the thirty-six Mediterranean prawns were for him; how many did I want? I have never seen anyone eat that many.

My second memory is of a never-to-be-repeated experience. Deep Purple had broken up and Ritchie Blackmore had gone on his own with a heavy metal band known as Rainbow. For some reason, during the settlement negotiations I was invited to a Rainbow concert at the Finsbury Odeon, the scene of seat slashing at Bill Haley concerts twenty years previously. I had been to rock concerts before, but never anything like this. The noise of the heavy metal band was indescribable. Being tortured as a terrorist at Guantanamo Bay had nothing on the agony in my ears. I will be amazed if heavy metal concert goers of the 1970s are not stone deaf today.

Elton John was another major artist who came to the firm because he was in dispute with his manager. I had no direct involvement but was aware of the libel case he brought against *The Sun* newspaper, which had made allegations both of his mistreating his dogs and having sex with rent boys. What is well known is that the case was settled and *The Sun* ran a huge front-page story that they had made up with Elton. What is not so well known is how this occurred.

The partner who was handling the case told me that when it became clear they were going to lose, *The Sun* had offered to settle. My colleague asked for £1 million in damages plus costs. Rupert Murdoch was patched by telephone into the settlement talks. My colleague told me that when asked by Rupert Murdoch how he justified £1 million compensation, he gave two reasons. In the first place, if Jeffrey Archer was worth £500,000 in his recent successful libel case, Elton John was worth twice that. Secondly, if *The Sun* ran the story as an exclusive front page on that Monday morning, the extra copies sold would more than compensate the newspaper for the damages. So that is what happened.

Years later I came across Elton John again. I was invited to a record industry event to celebrate his life. After a magical performance by Elton we heard a tribute by Bernie Taupin, who writes all Elton's lyrics. Bernie came up with the memorable line 'I don't fancy men or shopping'.

The 1960s were a period of significant investment in UK industry from the United States. Clearly, the new entrants had no traditional attachment to the major City law firms, so Frere Cholmeley was able to develop a clientele of major US corporations.

For fifteen years or so I found myself travelling regularly to the United States, primarily to New York or California. In those days, inevitably the client was expected to pay for first-class travel. At the beginning, Pan Am was the airline of choice, before it collapsed into bankruptcy. Pan Am flew Boeing 747s across the Atlantic Ocean and the upper deck was used as a restaurant for first-class passengers. So after take-off you went upstairs to sit down for drinks and food – a luxury now long gone. One of my clients was a keen backgammon player and on one occasion, returning from New York, after lunch upstairs I won a considerable sum as we hurtled through the air.

A few years later British Airways introduced Concorde flights to New York. The advantage of Concorde was that you could leave London in the morning and, flying at supersonic speed, arrive in New York for a meeting the same morning. The disadvantage was that the plane was small, rather uncomfortable and extremely expensive, so the passengers were bankers, film stars, the super-rich and professionals like us, whose clients were prepared to pay.

On Concorde you did from time to time sit next to the famous. On one occasion I sat next to the tennis star Martina Navratilova, who was rather taciturn but impressed me physically with the huge muscle that ran down her left arm from the elbow to the wrist. But my highlight was sitting next to the film star Michael Douglas. Just before the doors shut, a shambling figure came down the gangway. I recognised Henry Kissinger, who had been President Nixon's Secretary of State. As he passed us, Michael Douglas

looked up and said, 'Hiya, kid.' Such, clearly, was the symbiotic relationship between Hollywood and United States
politics.

I found myself representing Warner Communications
and fell under the spell of Steve Ross. The development
of the company under his management was startling. As
a young man he had married the daughter of a funeral
home operator in Manhattan. Each funeral home had an
adjacent parking lot where the hearses were parked. Steve
persuaded his father-in-law to rent the parking lots to com-
muters to the city, which proved hugely successful. The
next move was to buy the virtually bankrupt Warner Brothers film studios and change the name of the company to
Warner. A recorded music business followed and by the
time I became involved Warner was one of the largest entertainment companies in the world.

There has been speculation as to the origin of the huge
salaries paid to United States company executives, a trend
followed in the United Kingdom once the banks and entertainment worlds became global. Steve Ross was certainly a
major contributor to this development. He realised that his
executives often missed out on signing an actor or recording artist because they resented the difference between the
executive's income and the income that would need to be
paid to sign up the artist. His solution was to give his senior executives large salaries and bonuses. The problem

was, of course, that executives in other listed companies thought that they should be treated the same way. What was understandable in an entertainment company was applied to a manufacturing company without the same justification, so the executive salary spiral started.

Although I did not know him well, I found him inspirational to deal with, as did all his staff and professional advisers. When he died a light went out of the company that was never replaced.

Warner Communications was responsible for my first encounter with Cecil Parkinson in 1983. Cecil had come to serious public notice as chairman of the Tory Party and a member of the Prime Minister's inner war Cabinet during the Falklands War. After successfully masterminding the Tory victory in the 1983 general election, he had become what was then called President of the Board of Trade in Mrs Thatcher's Cabinet.

I was representing Warner Communications in its attempt to merge its recorded music division with its competitor PolyGram, owned by Philips, the Dutch conglomerate. In August 1983, I was on holiday on a Bahamian island where Cecil had an apartment and it was arranged that I would see him to urge him not to refer the merger to the Monopolies Commission as he had the power to do.

I walked along the beach with the sun setting to the west and arrived at his apartment at the appointed hour.

Cecil was dressed in a casual shirt, tan trousers and loafers. I was greeted with, 'Come in, this has been the worst day of my life.' He then spent half an hour telling me the story of his relationship with Sara Keays, who had been pursued by a journalist that day, culminating in the journalist crashing into her car. He went on to describe his conversation with the editor of the journalist's newspaper, his attempt to kill the story and his distress at the situation. He had told the Prime Minister on election night in June that year about his relationship with Sara and, as a result, was not appointed Foreign Secretary. The press were now about to reveal details of the affair. When he told me that he had told the most important woman in his life, i.e. the Prime Minister, of the scandal about to engulf him, and was telling his wife that evening, I felt I should interrupt and ask him if he should be telling me this as an active member of another political party, as I was by then. He retorted that he was telling me as a solicitor not a politician. His grasp of the rules of legal privilege was clearly shaky but I took the point. We had no discussion about the merger that had been the purpose of my visit, but in any event, negotiations between the parties foundered later that year so no merger took place.

The Cecil Parkinson–Sara Keays story exploded at the October Tory Party conference, resulting in Cecil's resignation. As someone put it, he was 'the first Cabinet minister to resign for staying with his wife'. I said nothing, not wishing to exacerbate his problems.

Next year I saw him in the street in the same Bahamian island. He thanked me profusely, and I asked him why. 'Because you never said anything after our conversation last year.'

We have got on well since, although I am not sure he really likes the Liberal Democrats or approves of the coalition. In the 1980s whenever we bumped into each other he always asked me, 'Are you one of us?' I had to remind him I was not. I suspect that before his personal difficulties, Cecil was Margaret Thatcher's favourite successor.

I also owed my Atari experience to Warner Communications. Atari started as a California-based creator and distributor of arcade games and by the early 1980s had seen the opportunity to expand into the newly developing personal computer market. Warner Communications had bought it in the 1970s and initially Atari was so successful that it represented about one third of the group profits. I was asked to represent it in Europe and indeed went on the board of its European company.

My first transaction involved buying back the exclusive United Kingdom distribution rights from Gerald Ronson, who – wisely, with the benefit of hindsight – did not believe the Atari hype. For a period I travelled regularly to California for meetings. Regular first-class travel had become seductive. I was staggered that my hosts seemed to start work at 7 a.m. having partied until the early hours. It was only later that one of them pointed out to me that cocaine enabled you to do that. That was not for me.

I suspect it was not drugs that caused the collapse of the business in the early '80s but overexpansion, coinciding with the development of competitive personal computers. Nevertheless a number of executives I knew went into rehab.

I did not accept the offer to become their General Counsel, however tempting life in California or regular first-class travel might have been. The last vestige of two heady years with Atari was the 'Pac Man' arcade machine located in the firm's basement, a source of much evening pleasure for overworked young lawyers.

Warner Communications also cured me of any penchant for pornography. *Playboy* magazine and *Penthouse* were just starting and Warner Communications, still known as Kinney, bought a Leicester-based company, Thorpe and Porter. Thorpe and Porter published soft porn, no more than would be standard in men's magazines today or indeed on Channel 5. As a young lawyer I spent six months reviewing each edition to advise whether anything should be deleted as potentially illegal. That experience cured me for good of any desire to look at a pornographic magazine.

Publishing was another area in which the firm developed expertise. I represented the United States publisher Harper & Row, now merged with Collins, trading as HarperCollins and owned by one of Rupert Murdoch's companies. It was through Harper & Row that I learnt of the story of codebreaking at Bletchley Park during the Second World War.

It is astonishing that until the early 1970s no history of the Second World War referred to the significant role played by Bletchley Park in decoding German ciphers, giving our troops after 1942 massive advantages in ground operations and enabling the navy to minimise the effect of U-boat attacks on shipping. It was not until 1974 that a book by F. W. Winterbotham was permitted by the intelligence services to reveal the impact of the Bletchley Park codebreakers.

Harper & Row wished to publish a follow-up to this story by Anthony Cave Brown but the intelligence authorities were blocking publication, so I was dispatched to see the redoubtable Admiral Denning, who chaired the relevant Whitehall committee responsible for issuing so-called D notices, which prevented publication of material thought to be inimical to our national security.

Norman Denning was the brother of Tom Denning, the Master of Rolls, and had made his name in wartime intelligence. I was summoned to see him at the Ministry of

Defence, the monolithic building off Whitehall that would not have felt out of place in communist Moscow. An amusing exchange ensued. The authorities were not concerned about the Bletchley Park story, as F. W. Winterbotham had made that public. They had two issues. First, undertakings had been given to French agents never to reveal their names. So we could not refer, for example, to Jean, a butcher living in Rue de Normandie, Rouen, as he could be identified. So the name could be changed to Robert, a baker, living in Rue de Bretagne, Rouen. Secondly, they were nervous that colonies to whom we had given independence would realise that the Enigma machines we had left with them would enable us to read their codes. Satisfactory alterations were made and the book was published.

Another avenue of potential growth for Frere Cholmeley was in Europe. I had a very early taste of the future when, as a young lawyer, I was asked to go as part of a team bidding for a manufacturing contract in what was then the USSR. Before my departure I received a visit from a shadowy figure who said he was from the Foreign Office. When I confirmed that I was going on the Moscow delegation, he gave me strict instructions to beware relationships with women, which would undoubtedly end with blackmail, and under no circumstances to answer the telephone if it rang in the middle of the night.

I was representing a consortium of companies who

were invited to Moscow to obtain a contract to establish and equip a factory for the Russians to manufacture textiles.

We stayed at the monolithic Hotel Russiya overlooking Red Square and our negotiations took place close by in one of the regime's office buildings. Over the next few days two things became clear. The only way we could tell if we were in the same office as the day before was by checking whether it was Lenin's picture on the wall or Stalin's, and my role was clearly unnecessary as the Russian delegation had no intention and probably no authority to alter their long, standard-form contract.

The highlight of our day was the compulsory fraternisation for half an hour that my Hungarian colleague Alex Nekam had described to me in Chicago some years previously. It was warm in July and we strolled through the garden at the rear of whatever office block we were in. On the second day's compulsory fraternisation, the leader of our team, the German Gerd Haller, asked his Russian counterpart how he had spent the Second World War. It emerged from their conversation that they had both been tank commanders, ending up at Stalingrad, and by their calculation had actually faced each other. Far from resulting in a resumption of hostilities, the atmosphere noticeably warmed and I suspect a better financial deal resulted for our side.

Sadly, I was not there for the final negotiations. At three

in the morning on the fourth day, the phone rang in my hotel room. I ignored the advice from the Foreign Office official and answered, to be told that my mother had died and they had been trying to reach me for a couple of days. I went back to London for the funeral, a sad occasion, particularly as my brother was only twelve years old.

The firm's European office expansion started slowly in the 1960s. An office in Paris was followed by one in Monaco and then Milan. As a young trainee solicitor, I was involved peripherally in the opening of the Paris office. My principal in the firm asked me if I would like to drive a hired lorry to Paris to deliver the furniture necessary for the new office, which had been purchased in London. I readily agreed and set off on the ferry – long before the days of the Channel Tunnel. All went well until I arrived in Paris. The office was in the Champs-Élysées. Nobody had explained to me that lorries were not allowed in the Champs-Élysées, so I was stopped. My confrontation with the police almost resulted in a night in a police cell.

But significant expansion occurred in the late 1980s. A year before the collapse of the Berlin Wall and the end of East Germany's Communist regime, we were invited to East Berlin to meet Herr Modrow, the East German Prime Minister. The office could have been in Moscow or any other Communist state. He asked us if we would set up an office in East Berlin. In anticipation of future unification of Germany he wanted to invite Western professional firms to East Germany to prepare their industry for Western methods, which were inevitably on the way. We explained that we had been trying for some months to obtain the necessary permits. He turned to an aide and instructed him to have the permit ready for collection the next day. So we opened the office and hired an Eastern German lawyer, Barbel Luther, to run it.

She suggested that we should have an opening party and booked a splendid room in the Centre for German–Soviet understanding on Unter den Linden. A group of us came over from London, stayed in a West Berlin hotel and went through the wall at Checkpoint Charlie to the party. We were somewhat stunned to mount a splendid staircase with large statues on either side, one of Stalin and one of Lenin, to a room full of the East Berlin establishment. We were talking about the late 1980s!

Sadly for us, but not for the East German population, our monopoly position did not last as long as we had hoped. The wall was demolished and the East German regime collapsed, so we were subject to competition from the West German legal profession.

A year later, Barbel Luther suggested we should have a further party to celebrate the anniversary of the opening of the office, and booked the same room. This time we stayed in East Berlin at the rather ornate Grand Hotel that the Japanese had built as a reward for contracts given by the East German dictator Erich Honecker. We walked to the same building, went up the grand staircase, noting that the busts of Stalin and Lenin had been removed, and entered the same room as before – now an Italian restaurant. Such was the speed with which East Berlin integrated into the Western world.

Nevertheless there were differences. Barbel Luther took me aside at the party to express a concern. She assumed that Frere Cholmeley had Jewish clients who would not wish to deal with German lawyers. I reassured her but realised that no West German lawyer had ever expressed the same view. Clearly the Communist regime had indoctrinated the East Germans with the belief that the Holocaust was their fault.

I also learnt to have a different perspective on the Second World War. When I went to Berlin for a management meeting I used to take the office staff out to lunch. One 14 February we were sitting in a local restaurant when, halfway through the meal, one of the secretaries said she had to leave as she had to prepare for her birthday party that evening. The rest of the table expressed their sympathies for her having her birthday that day. I was puzzled, as I would have assumed that Valentine's Day was a good day to have a birthday. After some embarrassment Barbel

Luther explained that 14 February was the day that Allied bombing had destroyed Dresden in 1945.

As someone brought up on a diet of war films where the Germans were the bad guys, I felt suitably humiliated.

Berlin also gave me my first taste of high-power politics through Edith Cresson, who was France's first and, to date, only female Prime Minister. On her introduction we were acting for the French oil giant Elf Aquitaine, who wished to buy the Leuna oil refinery, East Germany's largest refinery. After the collapse of Communism all the commercial assets of East Germany had been vested in a government agency, the Treuhand Anstalt, charged with disposing them to the private sector. So the negotiations were with the senior members of the Treuhand, who made it clear that Helmut Kohl, the German Chancellor, wanted the Elf Aquitaine bid to proceed. One afternoon as negotiations continued, the representative of the Treuhand was asked to take a call in the next room. On his return he announced that the UK Prime Minister, John Major, had telephoned to push for BP to be the purchaser. It was clear that the Germans had no intention of ignoring the wishes of Chancellor Kohl and the purchase by Elf Aquitaine went ahead.

Some years later it became apparent why this was the case. During an investigation in the mid-1990s into allegations of corruption and bribery by Elf Aquitaine's senior executives, a witness disclosed that to smooth the acquisition of the Leuna refinery, €256 million had been paid to Chancellor Kohl's political party, apparently cleared with President Mitterand.

This was clearly out of John Major's league, so BP had no chance and I realised why Britain often lost out on major overseas contracts.

A year later we took advantage of the collapse of Communism to open an office in Moscow. The city in 1991 was an extraordinary place. The most obvious indication of the arrival of capitalism was the popularity of a McDonald's restaurant. Even in the depths of winter, huge queues went round the block to gain admission when a table became available. A two-tier market operated, with vast price differentials between the world occupied by foreign businessmen and the standard of living of ordinary Muscovites. Ironically, one of the most expensive hotels in Europe was the National Hotel, which Lenin and Trotsky had occupied as their headquarters when they moved to Moscow from St Petersburg in 1917 before they took over the Kremlin.

It was against this background that we opened our office. The first person we hired to run it was Alexander Mamut. Alexander was a young, charismatic lawyer who took me round Moscow, a city very different from my previous experience. He told me that I had to understand that if you fixed a business meeting in Moscow only in about one out of ten cases would the meeting occur. Russia was in the process of developing a legal system that defined and protected the rights to property that the Communist system had denied. As nobody knew who owned the vast resources previously held by the state, there were huge opportunities for a Russian entrepreneur with a sharp eye to acquire assets cheaply. This was the period when the rise of the oligarchs began.

The harsher side of Russian life at that time was demonstrated by a conversation I had with a Russian client with whom I had become friendly.

In the early '90s I was on holiday in the south of France and discovered that he was staying nearby with a friend. We had lunch and he brought his friend, who was introduced as a former colonel in the KGB who had spent some years fighting with FRELIMO in Mozambique. After a sybaritic lunch he turned to me and told me that of course if I ever wanted anyone killed, I only had to contact his friend, who would oblige. I can assure readers that I have never taken him up on his offer, although it gave me an insight into subsequent events in Russia.

Alexander Mamut did not stay with us for too long, but went off to work for President Yeltsin in the Russian White House. I kept in touch, particularly as he wanted to educate his children in the United Kingdom. Some years later he asked to see me in London. 'I need some advice,

Tim. Where should I send my son to school? I understand you would not approve of Eton. How about Winchester?' I agreed, but have no idea who told him I would disapprove of Eton.

After Yeltsin, Alexander made a fortune in a mobile telephone business in Russia, but always maintained his links with the United Kingdom. He recently demonstrated his love for our country by buying and rescuing the Waterstones retail book chain. I understand he feels that as he has always liked book stores it would be fun to own them.

Alexander's successor in the firm's Moscow offices was a young Russian lawyer, Igor Shuvalov. Blond and engaging, Igor was anxious to learn all he could about Western legal systems and international transactions. I worked closely with him on the problems arising from a complex mining investment in Siberia by a listed Australian company, so got to know him well. It was clear to me that his ambitions would take him beyond legal practice, so it was no surprise to me that in 1997 he too went off to the Russian government. His rise has been rapid and at the time of writing he is the Senior Russian Deputy Premier, with wide responsibilities. As leader of the Russian delegation that outmanoeuvred England to be chosen to host the 2018 football World Cup, Igor accepted their victory with grace and humour.

Watching on television I had to pinch myself to realise

that this was the young lawyer who had joined us in his twenties all those years ago.

Over my years as a corporate lawyer I became more and more attracted to the business side of corporate activity. This really started in the early 1970s when I became involved with Malcolm Hawe. Malcolm had created a large private house builder, Marc Gregory Limited, over a short period of time. Malcolm was a man of huge charm and charisma and banks fell over themselves to lend multimillions. The gearing of the business was astronomical, but that was of course the period when the chief executive of NatWest could opine that the advantage of property was that it did not go down in value. He was wrong. The United Kingdom property bubble burst in 1973/4 and with the collapse in property value Marc Gregory could not meet its liabilities and was forced into liquidation. Malcolm Hawe and his colleagues had given personal guarantees to the banks, but these were not enforced, as far as I am aware.

Some years later Malcolm re-emerged to start another house-building business in the north-west, which was subsequently sold to AMEC plc for a considerable sum.

Although my dealings with Malcolm Hawe ended with the collapse of Marc Gregory, I was left with a fascinating legacy. My first legal involvement with his company had concerned a small listed property company, Greencoat Properties. Headquartered in Victoria in an eponymous

street, Greencoat Properties had started as an organisation
like Peabody, building cheap flats for London's workforce.
By the early 1970s the company had a small portfolio of
office and residential accommodation in the United Kingdom and had branched out with a number of residential
developments in France.

Under takeover panel rules then and now, anyone who
acquired 30 per cent or more of a public company had
to make an offer to the remaining shareholders at least at
the highest price paid to acquire the 30 per cent. Malcolm
Hawe's plan was to acquire 29.9 per cent in the market
and then to convene an extraordinary general meeting
to persuade the other shareholders to remove the board
and replace them with a Marc Gregory team, with me as
a non-executive director. The idea was to keep the listing and reverse Marc Gregory into Greencoat Properties.
This plan was agreed with Guinness Mahon, our merchant bank, and I left for a summer holiday. On my return
I was flabbergasted to be told by a jubilant Malcolm that as
he had been worried that we might not have the votes, he
had persuaded his friend Graham Pye, who ran another
house-building company, to buy some shares in Greencoat Properties. When I told him that we were in danger of
being seen to act in concert and would have to bid for the
whole company, I realised that he hadn't thought of that.

The takeover panel executive ruled against us so we

appealed to the full takeover panel. At the time, this was chaired by Hartley Shawcross, famous as the prosecuting counsel in the Nuremburg trials of the Nazi German hierarchy. When I gave evidence it certainly felt as if I was being prosecuted. We lost and were required to make an offer for the rest of the company. As Marc Gregory by then did not have the resources to fund the bid, we left the takeover panel offices in a seriously depressed state to walk back to our advisers, Guinness Mahon. We were delighted to meet a smiling Charles Villiers, their chairman, on the steps of the bank who told us that Guinness Mahon always supported its clients and that they would make the money available. This they did in partnership with Banque Belge, the Belgian bank.

The bid was made and as not all of the shareholders accepted we were able to retain the listing. Our slate of directors took over the board with the addition of two Guinness Mahon nominees. Plans to reverse Marc Gregory into Greencoat Properties foundered with the collapse of the former, at which Malcolm Hawe resigned as chairman, leaving two Marc Gregory executives, two Guinness Mahon nominees and me. So I became chairman, with the task of holding the ring between the two camps.

I also found myself thrown into the French business, I suppose because I was the only director who spoke or understood French and by then Frere Cholmeley had an

office in Paris. There were a few problems. The previous
board had embarked on a number of residential developments in France in partnership with an old-style property
developer, Anthony Somers. Somers was a larger-than-life
character who had made his fortune by buying portfolios
of mortgaged properties during the Second World War
and selling them for a huge profit when the war ended.
Indeed, in his book about property developers in the
United Kingdom, Oliver Marriott suggested that Somers
had made a fortune greater in real terms than any subsequent developer. Somers lived in great style in Charles
Street in Mayfair, looked after by an assistant, whom he
later discovered was stealing his money.

There were a number of problems with the deals the
previous board had done in France. First, the structure
was hugely advantageous to Somers. On each development, profits were to be split fifty–fifty but Greencoat
Properties supplied a guarantee to the bank providing
the funding. So in effect Greencoat Properties took all
the risk in return for only half the profits. My first task
was to extricate Greencoat Properties from the obligations under the bank guarantees. I managed to do this
with Somers's reluctant assistance. The second problem
was the nature of one of the developments. It became
clear to me that the operation was of the worst Rach-
manite nature. We owned a rundown tenement block and

Somers's idea was to persuade the tenants to vacate so refurbishment could take place and the flats could be sold off at a significant profit. The methods being used to persuade tenants to vacate were appalling and I persuaded the Greencoat board that this was not a development we should be part of. Again, I agreed with a reluctant Somers that we should sell our share and he undertook to find a buyer. I was amazed to discover that an enthusiastic buyer was the Vatican. Clearly the Catholic Church had different standards from ours.

After these problems were dealt with I had fewer dealings with Somers, who remained a man of enormous energies. He took up skiing at the age of seventy-five and skied regularly. I last heard of him from a colleague who had seen him at Heathrow Airport, heading off to the Ivory Coast, where he said there were opportunities like those England used to have but no longer did.

Outside the ambit of Anthony Somers, Greencoat embarked on a residential development in the Languedoc on the southern coast of France. The development faced the well-known nudist colony on Cap d'Agde, which was not its only advantage. Although the development seemed profitable, an internal audit indicated that something was wrong. We realised that our French manager was involved in the scam known technically as teeming and lading, where delays in recording sales receipts in the books of the business enabled cash to be creamed off, we suspected into our manager's account.

We confronted the manager with our allegations and a satisfactory settlement was reached. Apart from receiving my first lesson in the problems of teeming and lading, I learnt another lesson that has always stayed with me: never embark on a transaction overseas unless you have a local partner or manager you can totally trust.

By far the biggest crisis in Greencoat's overseas ventures occurred a year or two after the takeover. Planning consent had been obtained for a development in Paris on the quai de Jemappes, near the Place de la Bastille. Under French law, grant of a planning consent could be overturned by decision of the Conseil d'État, the Supreme Court for administrative justice established by Napoleon Bonaparte in 1799. A group of ecologists challenged our planning consent in the Conseil d'État on the grounds that our development would damage the skyline. They won.

This decision placed huge strain on the company's finances and risked its financial viability, so all available avenues were explored, either to obtain a reversal of the decision or to receive adequate compensation. Guinness Mahon had by then merged with Lewis & Peat and the holding company was chaired by Lord Kissin. Harry Kissin was Russian by birth and had made a fortune in East–West trade. More importantly for us, he was close to the Labour government, having funded Harold Wilson's private office in opposition, with links to James Callaghan, who had become Prime Minister in 1976 on Harold Wilson's surprise resignation. Harry Kissin persuaded James Callaghan to lobby President Giscard d'Estaing on our behalf and a note was agreed and passed by James Callaghan to the French president. But no progress was made through the political route.

As French law provided for compensation to be paid for loss of planning consent in our circumstances, we were inundated with people who said that for a large upfront payment they would obtain our compensation. The most colourful was Philippe Junot, who was married to Princess Caroline of Monaco. He certainly produced no money for us, but did provide an amusing vignette. At a meeting in his apartment a colleague asked if he could use his lavatory. He was shown through his bedroom and he couldn't help but notice that there were his and hers pillows on their double bed embossed with their photographs. Their marriage did not last.

The property business is rightly acknowledged as not being totally honest. The days when local councillors granted planning consents to their friends in return for backhanders were pretty much brought to an end with the high-profile prosecution of John Poulson, T. Dan Smith and others. But other forms of dishonesty were still prevalent.

One example I became aware of involved a transaction by Greencoat Properties regarding a commercial property near Southampton. We discovered later that the other contracting party had interposed itself between Greencoat Properties and the ultimate purchaser, so had taken a slice of the profit that could have belonged to us. The intermediary company was called Gateau Hellas – Greek cake – and we were never clear who received slices of the cake, although we suspected but of course could never prove that one or two of our colleagues may have been involved.

Amid our travails in France a more exciting opportunity occurred. Geoffrey Ball, who had joined Greencoat full time from Marc Gregory, spotted the potential of the City of Aberdeen Land Association. This company was one of Scotland's oldest listed businesses and had existed for over a hundred years, generating a small profit from feu duties in Aberdeen. Feu duties were ground rents attaching to a property under the feudal system of property law applicable to Scotland. Geoffrey noticed that the company's balance sheet contained land at no value in the Aberdeen suburb of Cults, which would be ripe for housing development to meet the needs of workers flocking to Aberdeen to take advantage of the North Sea oil boom. So we persuaded Guinness Mahon that Greencoat should acquire a stake in the Aberdeen company and bid for the rest, as we would be required to do under takeover panel rules. Vavasseur, the city money broker, held a significant stake and I was dispatched to see Clive Hollick, then starting out in business, who subsequently built a huge media business, owning Anglia Television and the *Daily Express*, before becoming a Labour peer. We had already lined up Bill Tawse, the chairman of the Aberdeen company, to support our involvement and I knew the price we were prepared to pay. Clive had only two comments. First, was Bill Tawse happy? Second, he would need to clear our price with Jim. When he left the room to speak to Jim it dawned on me who Jim was: Jim Slater, then regarded as the guru of stock market investment. We had not appreciated that Jim Slater had any involvement with the Aberdeen company, although I suspect with hindsight he may have been funding Vavasseur.

So the deal was agreed: we bought the Vavasseur stake and made an offer to the remaining shareholders. Again, as not all shareholders accepted we kept the listing. Planning consent was obtained to build executive houses at Cults, in the teeth of opposition from Roy Thomson, the local Liberal Party councillor, later to be my colleague on the Liberal Democrat national executive committee, who bore me no hard feelings about what had happened.

Greencoat Properties then sold its stake in the company to a consortium put together by Geoffrey Ball, who left to develop the house-building business. The name was changed to CALA and over the years a successful business was built up in Scotland and the home counties of England. Geoffrey Ball took CALA private in 1999 in a management buyout funded by HBOS.

I became a non-executive director of CALA, a post I retained until 1999. For the first few years, board meetings were in Aberdeen and I used to take the sleeper from King's Cross and wake up for breakfast as the train passed the beautiful stretch of coast between Edinburgh and Aberdeen.

It took me some time to grasp the complexities of Scottish attitudes. It seemed to me that the Aberdonians were insular and cared little for Scots from Edinburgh or Glasgow. People I met in Edinburgh were generally pro the union but hated Glasgow, which they thought, with some justification, was run by a socialist mafia. Glaswegians hated the English.

But the intensity of Scottish nationalism in the broadest sense was brought home to me by Andy Irvine, the famous Scotland and British Lions rugby star. He had retired from rugby and had become a partner in a leading Edinburgh firm of chartered surveyors. I was invited to play in a golf day and drew him as my partner. On the course, he exhibited the drive to win he had learnt on the rugby field. Off the course, over a drink, he told that the day had been a great day: England had lost at football and cricket and, I seem to remember, at tiddlywinks, which I had not appreciated involved international competition. Neither match was against Scotland. That did not matter as long as England lost.

By the 1980s it was clear that there was no real future for small listed commercial property companies. To grow you needed more capital, either through equity funding or bank debt and neither was available in any size to make a difference. Peter Goldie had joined the board as a Guinness Mahon nominee, but in 1983 wanted to leave Guinness Mahon to set up his own financial services business. He was to be joined by Cameron Brown, a colleague from the bank. I suggested that they should do this as a part of Greencoat Properties and they agreed. So Greencoat Properties now added Brown Goldie Ltd to its repertoire and changed its name to Abaco Investments so as to be top of the alphabetical list of quoted companies.

The real breakthrough came from a chance meeting in the street between Peter Goldie and John Gunn. John Gunn was at the time a high-flying City financier. His success started with the growth of the money broker Exco and he had been invited to join British & Commonwealth Shipping, controlled by the Cayzer family, to diversify the business away from its shipping background. Peter knew John because in his Guinness Mahon days he had raised the funding for John's development of Telerate, an onscreen information system that had been hugely successful. Peter quickly persuaded John that British & Commonwealth should take a stake in Abaco, recognising that John Gunn's reputation would give us a touch of magic and significantly move the share price.

In one of life's coincidences, it is one of John Gunn's daughters who become my agent, encouraged me to write this book and sadly died suddenly before it was published. I owe her huge thanks and so wish she had lived to see her idea realised.

John Gunn's involvement had the desired effect and in the mid-1980s we embarked on an acquisition spree to build a diversified financial services business. The trick was to create a virtuous circle, using our shares to make an acquisition, which then drove up the share price, enabling us to make another acquisition and so on. By the time we sold the company in the late '80s the market value of Abaco Investments had increased from £5 million to £90 million by this technique.

Our first acquisition was John Charcol, a mortgage broker run by John Garfield and Charles Wishart. I had tried to persuade Geoff Ball at City of Aberdeen Land to buy John Charcol, but the chemistry between the three of them did not work. Abaco was a different story. The plan was to buy a chain of estate agents, which would also provide mortgage services through John Charcol. So, starting with the well-known firm Hamptons, we acquired large numbers of firms throughout England. Indeed, at one time in the mid-1980s we were probably the largest estate agency firm in the United Kingdom.

On the back of our success in acquiring John Charcol and the agencies, we also built a large firm of chartered surveyors, Lambert Smith Hampton, and became major loss and average adjusters as well as big reinsurance brokers.

These were a heady two or three years for me, when I was both chairman and manager of the legal team doing the work on the acquisitions. To avoid stamp duty, many of the transactions were completed in either Amsterdam or Paris, where the opportunity was taken to invite the vendors of the companies we were buying, who were becoming our employees, to make them feel integrated in the group.

Memories of wild nights of celebration remain. But I suppose the most vivid memory is quite different. Peter Goldie and I were in Amsterdam to complete the purchase of a loss adjuster, which was owned by two shareholders of Middle Eastern background who had fallen out. In the course of the negotiations we had offered a slightly higher price to one than to the other. It was made absolutely clear to us that we must not disclose to the other party what we had done. We stayed in the Amstel Hotel, probably Amsterdam's premier hotel. We completed the first transaction at a higher price in one room and then

went to the other room to complete the second transaction at the slightly lower price. When we appeared,
the vendor told us that he was not prepared to complete
unless we disclosed how much we were paying the other
vendor. When we told him that first we had agreed with
the other vendor not to tell him and second he was con-
tractually obliged to complete, he suggested that he had a
gun in his briefcase and unless we told him he proposed
to shoot us. At that moment we needed our best negotiation skills. Eventually I calmed him down and undertook
that so long as he completed first I would tell him. He
did. I did. We survived.

Relationships with the vendors of companies we
acquired were often tricky. People who were used to running their own businesses did not always take easily to
public company discipline. Some of them clearly resented
the relatively young Abaco management team. In one
instance, we had acquired an insurance broking business
chaired by John Shipton, who I realised did not care for
me much. The extent of his dislike only became apparent
to me many years later.

In the late 1980s he was the president of the Cresta
Run in St Moritz, the famous tobogganing course. He
kept encouraging me to come and go down the course.
'A fit young chap like you can manage it from the top.' A
friend told me recently that beginners have to start from

halfway down. Had I followed his instruction I could have been killed or seriously injured. Fortunately, I never tried.

To build a diverse business so quickly depends on a number of strong personalities. We certainly had them. David Houghton had been recruited from Canada Life to run the property business, which we eventually sold to him and his colleagues in a management buyout when the property business became a relatively insignificant part of the group. Tall and exceptionally affable, David makes no enemies, a rare characteristic in his world. Peter Goldie was a life force. Always immaculately dressed with a bow tie, Peter was bald at a young age and rather saturnine in looks. He had a cerebral approach to business. It was no surprise when he left the business world some years later that he took a philosophy degree at Oxford and ended up as Professor of Philosophy at Manchester University. He died far too young. Peter's cerebral approach required balance in what was essentially a people business, and that balance was provided by his colleague from Guinness Mahon, Cameron Brown. Cameron is very much a people person and was highly adept at washing out the grit Peter Goldie sometimes threw in colleagues' eyes.

As the business started to grow, it was run as a triumvirate by Peter, Cameron and David. But, as with Octavian, Mark Antony and Lepidus, one of them had to become chief executive to ensure clear lines of responsibility. With

David's support and Cameron's acquiescence, Peter was appointed.

This situation did not last long, as Peter was persuaded to join British & Commonwealth as chief executive and Cameron took over.

Once Peter took over at British & Commonwealth it was clear that Abaco's days of independence were numbered. After an abortive attempt to bid in 1987, which foundered in the stock market collapse, British & Commonwealth came back with a revised offer in 1988. As they already held 29.9 per cent, any reasonable bid would clearly succeed. As Peter Goldie and John Gunn were conflicted as directors of Abaco, negotiations were entrusted to Paul Myners, then head of Gartmore, a British & Commonwealth subsidiary. I would not have predicted that many years later Paul and I would face each other across the floor in the House of Lords, when Paul became City Minister under Gordon Brown. Paul, Cameron and I met over a weekend in the Inn on the Park hotel by Hyde Park Corner and agreed a price of 72 pence per share, which we felt was pretty good. So did the Abaco board the next day we met. Abaco board meetings took place at St Helen's Place in the City, later to be flattened by an IRA bomb. We asked Peter Goldie and John Gunn to leave the room and agreed to accept the offer in five minutes of conversation. I suggested to the board that we couldn't ask Peter and

John to come back into the room so quickly as they would think our speedy acceptance meant that they had offered too much. So we talked among ourselves for half an hour.

The Abaco experience certainly gave me a taste for business rather than the law and this interest was enhanced when I became involved in a mining business in Russia.

In the early '90s we were asked to represent Star Mining, an Australian listed company who had acquired a minority stake in a Russian company, Lenzoloto, who had a massive undeveloped gold resource in Siberia. Mark Twain once memorably said that a gold mine was a hole in the ground with a liar standing over it. That was certainly confirmed in reverse by our experience in Russia, where, notwithstanding our possession of a signed decree by Prime Minister Gaidar confirming our rights of ownership and our expenditure of nearly $50 million to start developing a plant, the Russian government challenged our ownership and cancelled our investment.

Despite Mark Twain, the mining business certainly attracts powerful characters.

Few are more powerful than Malcolm Turnbull, who joined the Star Mining board. An ex-Rhodes scholar from Oxford, where he was a contemporary and friend of Benazir Bhutto, Malcolm was fresh from his cross-examination of Lord Armstrong in the Spycatcher case in Australia, where he elicited an admission that Lord Armstrong had

not been lying but had been economical with the truth –
a phrase that is now lodged in the vernacular. I witnessed
Malcolm's toughness when he told me that his young son
had not wanted to learn to swim so he simply threw him
in the swimming pool to sink or swim. Malcolm certainly
has a tendency to fall out with people, so I was amazed
when he was later elected leader of the Liberal Party in
Australia and much less surprised when he was subsequently ousted.

Rudolph Agnew, now Sir Rudolph, was a different
animal. He had steel and charm in equal proportions as
chairman of Star Mining. His steel showed at the company's annual meeting in Sydney when he told a shareholder
who questioned his salary that if he didn't like it he could
take over his job. Knowing his charm, I was surprised
on meeting him at Heathrow to travel to Sydney to be
told that under no circumstances would he sit next to me.
I realised why when he smoked endless cigarettes on the
non-smoking flight, much to the irritation of nearby passengers. When I asked him how he managed this he told
me that he had a letter in his pocket from the chairman of
British Airways allowing him to smoke.

It was some years later that I discovered from Michael
Young the key role Rudolph had played in the abolition of
apartheid in South Africa. Michael Young had been chief
of staff to Ted Heath as Prime Minister and then joined

the Liberal Democrats, where I met him. When Willie
Whitelaw resigned as the Member of Parliament for Pen-
rith in 1987, Michael narrowly failed to win the ensuing
by-election and, in the early 1990s, joined Consolidated
Gold Fields.

Hostility to the apartheid regime was a key part of my
early life. At university we had boycotted bank accounts at
Barclays due to their involvement in South Africa. We had
no doubt that Peter Hain had been framed by the South
African security services, known as BOSS, when he was
accused of robbing a bank in Putney, as punishment for
his activities in anti-apartheid organisations. I certainly
believed the South African High Commissioner when she
told me years after the collapse of the apartheid regime
that she had no doubt from her time in Scandinavia that
the Swedish Prime Minister Olof Palme had been assassinated by BOSS. But it was Michael Young who explained
to me how critical Rudolph's role had been.

Rudolph was chairman of Consolidated Gold Fields
and was persuaded by Michael that the company had a
significant interest in ensuring a peaceful political transi-
tion in South Africa, rather than a violent revolution in
which their assets would be at risk. Rudolph authorised
Michael to set up deniable talks between the ANC and
representatives of the South African government. This
he did, with talks taking place at a safe house in Mells,

Somerset, with Thabo Mbeki representing the ANC and an Afrikaner representing the government. When Mbeki succeeded Nelson Mandela as President, this Afrikaner became his close adviser.

The talks dragged on until President de Klerk took office, Mandela was released and the framework discussed at Mells was implemented.

I am clear that neither Rudolph nor Michael Young have obtained proper credit for this achievement other than in the film made by David Aukin for Channel 4. Indeed, Michael told me that he could not even find a plane seat for Mandela's funeral.

—CHAPTER SEVEN—

LOCAL GOVERNMENT

I T WAS MY experience in the mining industry that
acted as the catalyst to make me leave the law in 1995,
establish a corporate finance boutique, develop a portfolio life in business and devote more time to my political
career. I was by then heavily involved in Liberal Democrat policies.

Although brought up in a fiercely political family, I did
not become involved in Oxford politics and indeed was
rather contemptuous of those who did. In 1967, I was still
living in my parents' house after my mother had died while
I finished my articles at Frere Cholmeley. I was asked if I
would join the local Liberal Party and was signed up, little

realising what this would lead to. I was reluctantly persuaded to attend the annual general meeting of the Acton Liberal Party the next week, as they were concerned that otherwise there would not be the necessary quorum.

When the chairman of the meeting called for nominations for officers, the number of people attending the meeting equalled the number of vacancies, so I found myself elected vice chairman. They told me not to worry as I would not have much to do. They were wrong.

Shortly afterwards, Bernard Floud, the Labour Member of Parliament for Acton, was uncovered as a Czech spy and committed suicide, thereby triggering a by-election.

Acton had been fairly moribund for the Liberal Party so the first decision was whether a Liberal candidate would be fielded at all. A group of grandees from the Liberal Party came to Acton to interview us to see whether it was worthwhile putting up a candidate. There were only five or six of us, all under thirty, but our enthusiasm won them over. After all, it had been only five years since Eric Lubbock's victory in the Orpington by-election with a huge swing to him. As it was a Labour-held seat, the convention was that Labour had to move the writ to fix the date of the election, and Labour would clearly delay this as they were at the height of their unpopularity. The plan was to use this delay to build up our organisation with help from other London constituencies.

We also had to find a candidate. Frank Davis was eventually persuaded to stand. Frank had been Mayor of Finchley before local government reorganisation had subsumed Finchley into the larger borough of Barnet. Frank had obtained significant publicity as mayor when a constituent complained that his rubbish had not been collected, which Frank dealt with by commandeering a rubbish collection van at the local depot and driving it personally to collect the complainant's rubbish.

After we chose Frank as our candidate I came up with an idea that later resulted in a change in the law. Up until then, a candidate's party affiliation could not appear on the ballot paper. This preserved the fiction that the candidate not the party was receiving the vote. So a huge amount of effort in any campaign went into reminding the electorate of the name of a party's candidate. This was a problem particularly for the Liberal Party, with fewer resources than the other two parties.

So I suggested to Frank that he change his second name to 'Liberal' so that he would appear on the ballot paper as 'Davis, Frank Liberal'. He agreed. So the Home Office changed the law afterwards. Whether they would have done so anyway I know not, but the prospect of candidates changing their second name to 'Labour' 'Conservative' or 'Liberal' would obviously have made a mockery of the restriction.

In the event it made no difference to the result. Frank came third with 11.5 per cent of the vote. Not a bad result in a Tory/Labour fight, but a lost deposit, as in those days the threshold was 12.5 per cent. Looking back to 1967, the campaign itself is a blur, but a few memories remain. Meeting Kenneth Baker, who won the seat for the Tories, for the first time and realising that he was destined for future greatness; being sent to spy on a public meeting due to be addressed by Denis Healey and discovering no one else there; and the actions on the night of the count of an independent candidate of Asian origin who, when the result was announced, jumped off the town hall balcony and survived. I do remember canvassing a street where every household was Irish. In those days and – sometimes even now – in an Irish household if the wife answered the door she would call her husband, as he dealt with the politics of the house. The Liberal Party at that time was unpopular with the right-wing press for the principled stand taken in Parliament to oppose the government's restriction on Kenyan and Ugandan Asians coming to Britain, in breach of undertakings given in the independence negotiations. After five consecutive Irishmen had bitten my head off for wanting all those foreigners to come here, I snapped at the sixth door.

I asked my verbal assailant where he came from. On being told 'County Cork', I asked him why he had any more right to be here than an East African Asian. He slammed the door in my face but I did feel better.

I certainly drew a number of lessons from my first political campaign. Don't waste your time when canvassing in trying to convert the bigoted. Only answer back occasionally to make yourself feel better. More seriously, public meetings in elections in urban seats were becoming a waste of time and resources. Most importantly, in any by-election the Liberal Party must try to define itself in the public eye as the only real challenger to the incumbent. Otherwise we would be squeezed out by the other parties.

But I had been seriously bitten by the political bug, a bite that has never left me.

That was also the year of the London borough elections and I was persuaded to stand for Ealing Council in East Ward, which straddled the A40 at the east end of the borough of Ealing, abutting White City and Shepherd's Bush. It was a three-member ward, which we had no chance of winning, but we gave it a go. In an early example of the practice of community politics, I encouraged and helped to organise a tenants' association on a large council estate at the heart of the ward. Sadly for me, but not for them, my attempt to encourage a rent strike until maintenance was improved failed to obtain support, so the desired publicity did not result. I also spent time on Saturdays signing up potential supporters as Liberal

Party members. This was reasonably successful, probably as I was not always scrupulous in telling people what we stood for. I remember signing up an Australian woman who joined because she had been a member of the Liberal Party in Australia. I did not tell her that the Liberal Party in Australia was the Conservative Party. In the election we came seventh, eighth and ninth behind three Labour and three Tory candidates. My position as seventh was entirely to do with my position on the ballot paper. The other candidates' surnames were Roylance and Scherer so as Razzall I was the first Liberal. The year of 1968 was disastrous for Labour in London, with the Tories even winning control of Islington Council, and the Liberal Party's performance was dismal. The general secretary of the London Liberal Party told me that he felt it was virtually impossible for us to win a seat in a London borough election.

So I threw myself into developing my legal career, moved from Acton to Westfields Avenue in Barnes, had two children – Katie and James – and had no political involvement for the next five years. Then I met John Waller at the party of a mutual friend. John was already a local celebrity, as, contrary to the predictions of the secretary of the London Liberal Party, he had won a council by-election in Richmond Town ward, intriguingly beating my friend Bob Marshall-Andrews, who later became a Labour MP. John's career was in computers, and he had been commissioned to establish the computer system for the insurance company owned by Emil Savundra. When the date approached to go live, Savundra had asked John whether it was ready. When told that it was probably 95 per cent finished, that is, almost there, Savundra said that it was ideal and went live. So all of the premium income came in but failure to pay out a claim could be blamed on the computer system. John of course was totally unaware of this. Savundra was later convicted of fraud.

John ate, slept and breathed Liberalism and is a man of huge energy. He desperately wanted to be a Member of Parliament and, having failed to be chosen as the candidate for Richmond in October 1974, moved to Twickenham and stood twice there unsuccessfully in the seat later won by Vince Cable.

The house he bought in Twickenham had a long garden backing on to the Thames, in which John often bathed.

His energy has clearly not abated. I last saw John in Corfu in 2010 when walking out to field for a Jonathan Marland team. John rushed to intercept us, waving copies of his book, which he said was outselling Gerald Durrell in Corfu bookshops. Indeed, I hear he put a photo of me bowling in his latest book.

It was John who persuaded me to put my name forward to fight Mortlake ward in the May 1974 election. To encourage me, he said that Chris Graham would be running the campaign. Chris Graham was in his mid-twenties and was already famous in Liberal Party circles, as he had been elected to Liverpool Council while still an undergraduate at Liverpool University. Chris had a cerebral approach to politics; I remember him once telling me that his favourite way to spend Saturday afternoon was writing a strategy paper for the development of the constituency. But he certainly knew how to produce leaflets. Later he failed in his attempt to become a Member of Parliament in the West Country and, after a successful career at the BBC, became director general of the Advertising Association and is now Sir Christopher Graham, the Information Commissioner.

Mortlake ward at that time stretched from Barnes High Street in the east to the South Circular Road in the west and from the river Thames in the north to the railway in the south. In later years, after a boundary review, Mortlake ward was extended to Manor Road to the west. I lived in a terraced house in Westfields Avenue in an area that, as it became 'gentrified', came to be known as 'little Chelsea'.

In 1974, several years before the right to buy enabled council tenants to buy their properties at a heavily discounted price, Mortlake ward had over 50 per cent council tenants and in the previous borough elections had voted overwhelmingly Labour, with the Liberals a poor third. A three-member ward, the leading Labour councillor, the Labour leader on the council, was Tony Hart, the husband of Judith Hart, the Labour Cabinet minister. Apart from me, the other two Liberal candidates were Rosemary Scott Owen, in her late twenties, who sold pharmaceuticals for a drug company, and Derek Wainwright, the oldest of us, who was the clerk to the Kensington magistrates.

The politics of the ward were clearly changing. In the previous year Stanley Rundle had captured the Greater London Council (GLC) seat for Richmond and had clearly obtained significant support in Mortlake. Gossips reported that when canvassing Chertsey Court, the mono-lithic council flat block on the A316 opposite the Mortlake cemetery, Tony Hart had been heard to moan that Chert-sey Court seemed to be going Liberal. The night before the count, which took place on the Friday morning, we had a celebratory dinner in a restaurant just off Mortlake High Street. Chris Graham told me that he thought we had won, but it would be close. We had and it was. We had overturned a massive Labour majority. Even better, we had elected ten councillors in the borough: the three of us in Mortlake, Stanley Rundle and two colleagues in Kew, John Waller and two colleagues in Richmond Town and David Williams in Ham & Petersham. We were ten out of twenty or so Liberals elected across London, which was regarded as so significant that Jeremy Thorpe invited us all to tea at the House of Commons. How low our sights were set in those days!

So I started my career as a Mortlake councillor, which ended only when I stood down in 1998.

The leader of our ten-strong group was Stanley Rundle, an extraordinary man in every way. His electoral achievements were huge. He had been elected a councillor in Kew in 1966 at a time when Liberals did not get elected as councillors in London boroughs; he lost his seat in 1968 but was re-elected in a by-election in 1969. He had won the GLC election in 1973, fought on the parliamentary constituency boundaries, and had come a good second to the Tory MP Anthony Royle in the February 1974 general election.

The secrets of his success are easy to see with hindsight, but were revolutionary at the time. Stanley was one of the pioneers of communicating with the electorate through the electoral cycle, not just during election campaigns. In 1963 he started and regularly distributed *Kew Comment*. This covered local issues, stating what the problem was, how it had come about and what was to be done – laced with some modest self-promotion and finishing with an invitation to the reader to get in touch if the problem recurred. Although *Kew Comment* seems dated fifty years later, this approach formed the inspiration for the now ubiquitous focus leaflet.

Of course, Stanley had huge charisma. An early example came at a packed public meeting protesting against

the endless lorry traffic going in and out of a site in Kew
on the South Circular Road. An irate resident stood up
and shouted that if this didn't stop he would lie down in
the entrance to block lorries coming in. Quick as a flash,
Stanley stood up and said that if he was going to do this
he should ring him, and he would be the first to join him.

His charisma was later in evidence in sadder circumstances. After the February 1974 general election, Stanley
had been readopted to fight the seat in the next election,
which was anticipated soon. Unfortunately, Stanley had
become seriously ill and a meeting of the Richmond executive was called to cross-question Stanley as to whether he
would be fit enough to fight. Instead of downplaying his
illness, Stanley stood up and recounted all his ailments in
the goriest detail, while confirming that he fully intended
to fight the election. Well, that's OK then, we all said. What
a magician!

Stanley's professional expertise was in languages. He
helped to compile a definitive English–Italian dictionary
for the Cambridge University Press and claimed to have
a working knowledge of thirty-three languages. His personal life could only be described as eccentric. He lived
in Kew with his wife and secretary, who was called Joan
Rundle, although she wasn't his wife, sister or daughter.
Only the Rundles knew the real basis of this arrangement.
Unfortunately, despite Stanley's virtuoso performance at

the executive committee, his health worsened and he was
forced to withdraw as our parliamentary candidate. He
died a few years later. I have always felt that Stanley has
never had the credit he deserved as a pioneer of Liberals
in local government.

When I was first elected, the Tory leader of the council
was Harry Hall, very much a town boss in the traditional
style. After council meetings, drinks and canapés were
served in the town hall to councillors and their guests.
On these occasions Harry Hall seemed to enjoy talking
to the young Liberals and spreading his political wisdom.

Two things particularly spring to mind. He was talking
to a group of us and disclosed that he had found that the
best handbook for a leader of the council was Machiavelli's
The Prince. On another occasion we were chatting and I
told him that there seemed to be a lot of infighting in his
Tory group and assumed he would be watching his back.

'Oh no, Tim,' he replied, 'in the Tory Party we stab
each other in the front.' I suspect Margaret Thatcher would
have agreed with him after her departure from Downing
Street.

It took nine years from May 1974 to obtain control of
Richmond Council. In 1978 the Tories won thirty-four
seats to our eighteen and in 1982, fighting in alliance with
the newly formed SDP, we won twenty-six seats to the
Tories' twenty-six, but they had elected the mayor so

retained control with his casting vote. Then, in November 1983, we won a council by-election in Hampton Wick ward and obtained control. At the time the only other councils controlled by the party were Adur and Hereford, Liverpool having been lost a few years earlier.

As Richmond was the forerunner of our success in local government over the next twenty-five years, it is reasonable to ask the questions 'why Richmond?' and 'why Richmond before other similar areas?' The first electoral lesson, which I had learnt all those years before in Oxford, was to ensure that in a three-party competition the Liberal Party had to become the only challenger to the ruling party. So in Richmond this meant eliminating the Labour Party as an opposition party to the Tory regime. In later years, the converse was true in places like Liverpool or Newcastle, where the Liberal Democrats had to replace the Tories as the alternative to the controlling Labour Party.

The next factor was undoubtedly the sociological changes that were occurring. As we won the wards that had previously been won by the Labour Party, it was clear that increasing prosperity had changed the political attitudes of the families who had traditionally voted Labour. The men were increasingly less dominated by the trade union loyalty to Labour. The women were emerging from decades of subservience and poverty to appreciate politicians who related to them when it came to neighbourhood

amenities and the local school for their children, and, most
importantly, who tried to consult them about the issues that
most affected them and their families. At the other end of
the economic scale, an appeal to social conscience played
well in the large houses in Barnes, Richmond and Kew.

A number of our supporters in Mortlake demonstrated
these changes. Ron Reeves and his wife Joan were stal-
warts from the Manor Grove council estate. Ron had been
a shop steward for his union and had always voted Labour.
He was straight from the traditionally working-class background of his generation, was fiercely patriotic and firmly
loyal to his friends and family. I quickly realised that if the
Rons of this world were coming over to us, there was no
limit to how many votes we could muster from Labour.
Ron and his wife Joan helped to deliver the vote in their
polling district in election after election.

Mrs Mac was someone different. She lived in one of
the block of flats on Mortlake High Street and was known
to all as Mrs Mac. She had fostered innumerable children,
many of whom kept in touch with her. Of Scottish origin,
she had been a member of the Communist Party – not
many left by the mid-1970s – and was one of the most lov-
ing and caring people I have known. After initial caution
at these middle-class interlopers, she did vote for us but
would never become a member, as she felt it would be
betraying her Communist roots.

Win Florey lived in Waldeck Terrace, in the heart of old Mortlake. Win was in her seventies when I first met her and we quickly signed her up as a member. Win came from a poverty-stricken background. She told me that she had been brought up with her brothers and sisters in two rooms in St Leonards Road in East Sheen. Like Mrs Mac, Win had a heart of gold and in her eighties was still doing the shopping for neighbours much younger than her. I have always remembered Win's instructions to me later in her life: 'Don't believe them, Tim, if they talk about the good old days. They were not!' A lesson UKIP might do well to take on board.

The sociological changes in the area meant that celebrities were starting to move in. We were told that a singer in Jethro Tull lived at the end of my road, but whenever I knocked on his door when canvassing he wasn't in, or never answered, maybe because he disliked Liberals. Tim Rice, fresh from his triumph with *Jesus Christ Superstar*, lived on Barnes Terrace, overlooking the river. I canvassed him several times and despite swapping cricket anecdotes – he is a passionate cricket fan – I failed to move him from his commitment to the Tories. I found him surprisingly right-wing and was not totally surprised when he recently announced he had made a donation to the UK Independence Party.

Alan Price was another matter. His origins were in

Jarrow and he told me with pride that his father had been on the famous Jarrow March on London against unemployment during the depression. His original claim to fame had been as the moving spirit behind The Animals and particularly their hit song 'The House of the Rising Sun'. He became a firm supporter and many a happy hour was spent with Alan over a drink – or two or three – in local restaurants.

At one stage we tried to involve Alan in creating a theme song for an election campaign, but it never quite happened.

Undoubtedly we were at the start of the community politics revolution. Community politics infected our political life with a resolution proposed at the Liberal Party Assembly at Eastbourne in 1970 by Gordon Lishman and Bernard Greaves – not to be confused with Tony Greaves, now a Liberal Democrat peer. The community politics approach had three related themes. First, if the Liberal Party wished to succeed it must build up its political base from the ground up, not from the top down. Second, this meant that politics should not just be conducted during an election campaign but should take place continuously. But third, the community politics approach had a clear philosophical underpinning. The basic method was to create and recreate communities, providing a range of mutual support for its members, creating opportunities to develop and establish a personal role and purpose in life, and, in cooperation and conflict with each other, providing the diversity and pluralism that should be the basis of mature, participatory democracy. So it is really only in small, geographically coherent neighbourhoods that people can take a direct part in the making of decisions and the exercise of power.

Our application of the principles of community politics to the London borough of Richmond had several strands. The reorganisation of London boroughs in the 1960s had emasculated local government by putting the principle of common size and identical powers before the recognition of perceived local communities. We realised from the start that the interests and concerns of the residents of Mortlake or Barnes would be different from those of the residents of Hampton Wick or Teddington. So our regular focus leaflets – we called them 'Comments' – were local to each community in name and topics.

Stanley Rundle had started holding what were called pre-council meetings – public meetings shortly before borough council meetings to enable members of the public to raise with their local Liberal councillors issues that concerned them. As we won more wards, this concept was applied more generally. 'Comments' invariably featured surveys asking for views on local issues, which could form the basis of campaigns for action. We encouraged local people to start community associations and our activists to become involved as enablers and participants. When we obtained a majority on the council we realised that it would be too expensive to revert to the local council offices in each area that had existed before local government reorganisation, so we came up with the idea of mobile offices – large caravans with systems linked to the central offices – which went to specific areas on specific days of the week, where local people could have their problems with the council resolved without having to travel to the borough offices in Twickenham.

We realised that we could use modern polling techniques to test residents' views on key local issues and in the 1980s we were among the first local authorities to employ the MORI polling organisation each year in the run-up to setting the Budget to test opinion as to the right balance between income and expenditure. We were somewhat startled at the opposition from the Tories, who claimed that no opinion poll could obtain an accurate view. We were vindicated when John Banham, the chair of the Audit Commission, wrote to the council's chief executive about our polling operation, saying he had seen the future and it worked.

We also mobilised local residents to become involved in campaigns on issues that affected them. In opposition, we could encourage campaigns against the Tory-run council. When we ran the council, it was harder. So in political

terms the Tory government was a better target. A good
example was the campaign we encouraged in the mid-
1980s against the government plan to reroute the South
Circular Road over Barnes Common. So large was the
public meeting we called to discuss the issue, in a draughty
church hall in Barnes, that when the meeting started there
were as many people outside as could fit in the hall. So
we held the meeting again an hour later for the second
group of protestors. I think this was my first brush with
central government, as I led a delegation of local councillors – cross-party – to see Peter Bottomley, who was then
a transport minister in Margaret Thatcher's government.
We travelled up to Westminster and were ushered into a
room with a long table where we sat on one side, with six
or so civil servants on the other, waiting for the minister.
There had recently been a number of nasty rapes on or
around Barnes Common by someone the tabloids were
calling the 'Barnes Common rapist'. When the minister
came in and asked what the meeting was about, he was
told 'Barnes Common'. I think my fellow councillors, all
women, were somewhat stunned to be greeted by the minister with, 'I didn't think anyone was interested in Barnes
Common except the rapist.' Shortly afterwards Margaret
Thatcher brought back Cecil Parkinson as Secretary for
State for Transport and he killed the scheme. The Barnes
Common rapist had been caught by then.

Of course, in electoral politics, community campaigning did not always pay dividends, as the proponents of community politics always recognised. A local campaign in Kew against the establishment of a 'bail hostel' resulted in the defeat of David Blomfield in the 1978 borough elections. David had succeeded Stanley Rundle as leader of our council group, so his loss was particularly unfortunate.

Sadly, as the years went by, community politics became less a system of ideas for social transformation and more a technique for winning elections. Liberals were derided as being obsessed by 'pavement politics'. At least concerns with potholes met the US politician Tip O'Neill's rule that all politics is local, in contrast to the Labour Party executive meetings in Richmond, where, we were told, endless discussions took place on what to do about Biafra. But by the 1990s what the Liberal Party had started in the 1970s was being copied by the other two parties nationally, so differentiation with them was harder to sustain.

Although the Liberal Party had always campaigned for reform of the electoral system, our experience in Richmond demonstrated how the unfairness of the system operated in our favour once we crossed a certain threshold. Despite the fact that we never obtained 50 per cent of the overall vote, in 1986 we won forty-nine seats, the Tories three and Labour none. In 1990, the result was forty-eight seats to us, four to the Tories and none to Labour. In the last election

I fought in 1994 we won forty-three seats, the Tories seven and Labour two.

Of course, despite our electoral success a number of areas remained solidly Tory. I remember canvassing Fife Road, a road next to Richmond Park with large detached houses. After the first ten houses, all of whom had told me that they were Tory and disliked the Liberal council, I thought I would have some fun. For the next ten houses I said I was conducting a consultation as to whether the name of Fife Road should be changed to Nelson Mandela Street. Margaret Thatcher had recently described Nelson Mandela as a terrorist, so the expressions on the doorsteps were stunned.

But whatever political philosophy or campaigning techniques we applied, our success could not have been achieved without the people who became key members of the council. I often felt that there was nothing particularly special about Richmond and Twickenham and that the same group of people could have won control of many other areas had we all found ourselves there. It is invidious to single out individuals but the contribution of David Williams (now Sir David) must be highlighted.

David is without doubt a political genius. Although for some time he was John Waller's partner in his computer business, in reality he has devoted all his adult life to politics. He was first elected to Richmond Council in 1974 as councillor for Ham & Petersham. On David Blomfield's defeat in Kew in 1978, as I indicated earlier, David was elected our group leader, with me as his deputy, positions we held unopposed until I stood down from the council in 1998.

Most politicians fall into two categories – those who are obsessed with minutiae and those who see the big picture. David is the rare political animal who does both. His memory for past experiences is legendary, his application of past experience to current problems is masterful and his ability to foresee problems before they arise is second to none.

David's political life has been devoted to local government, which led to his involvement with the Audit Commission and his knighthood. I fear that the party has never given him the national role from which it would benefit. Unfortunately, in David's case, May 2014 sadly demonstrated the truth of Enoch Powell's famous aphorism that all political careers end in failure. David lost the council seat in Ham & Petersham that he had held for forty years.

It is also relevant to ask why, after taking control of the council, it took another fourteen years before the party won the two parliamentary seats in the borough – Richmond and Twickenham. After all, in 1986, the year before the 1987 general election, we had won huge victories in the borough elections. On reflection, there were a number of factors that explained this apparent anomaly.

Anecdotally, we all knew people who told us that they

supported us locally but could not do so nationally. But far more significant was the difference in turnout. Although borough elections were hard fought, there were large numbers of people who took little interest in local issues but turned out in force to vote in general elections – in Richmond and Twickenham, primarily for the Tories. The significance of differential turnout was demonstrated in 2010, long after I had left Richmond Council. The general election that year coincided with the London borough elections and the turnout was 20 per cent higher than normal, so control of the council was lost on the back of a turnout to elect Zac Goldsmith as the Tory MP. Inevitably, despite our attempts to persuade the electorate that Richmond and Twickenham were different, we could not totally isolate ourselves from national trends. The year in which we won our first landslide council victory, 1986, was a poor year for the Tories everywhere. By 1987 the Tories were riding high in the polls and Margaret Thatcher could call the election at a favourable moment.

In 1992, we were the victims of the anti-Kinnock surge, particularly in the last week before polling day, when the Tories argued that votes for the Liberal Democrats would put Labour into Downing Street.

In 1997, John Major was boxed in as he had to call the election at the end of five years, with the polls reflecting the unpopularity of the Tory government. So for the first time since 1974 the general election took place in an anti-Tory environment, thus helping to victory Jenny Tonge in Richmond and Vince Cable in Twickenham.

Until 1997 a number of the party hierarchy and indeed the political press felt that local government success could not be converted into victory in parliamentary seats. But 1997 proved them wrong. Certainly in south-west London, in addition to Richmond and Twickenham, the success of Paul Burstow in Sutton & Cheam, Tom Brake in Carshalton and Ed Davey in Kingston was on the back of significant progress in local government elections.

Parliamentary by-elections can be won from scratch with little local government strength. Activists can be brought in from outside. But to win a parliamentary seat requires supporters, campaigners and leaflet deliverers already in place. These networks are normally built through local government success.

So, was the borough a better place after my fifteen years as deputy leader of the council? As chair of the Policy and Resources Committee, I presented fifteen budgets, so I saw at close hand the effect of central government clampdown on local government expenditure. When I was first elected in 1974, 75 per cent of the council's revenue was raised locally. By the time of my last budget, the percentage was reversed. So, inevitably, as the Treasury contributed so much, they wanted greater control over how the money was spent.

With hindsight I feel we had a number of great achievements. First, the capital improvement in and better maintenance of our council housing stock underpinned our electoral success in previously Labour areas. It is hard to believe that when I was first elected my ward still had properties with outside lavatories and a six-storey block of flats without a lift.

Second, we radically improved the school system. The Tories had introduced a comprehensive system in the borough, as clearly many of their middle-class supporters were concerned at the effect that eleven-plus failure had on their children. We soon realised that the improvement and development of the school system reflected our key beliefs. So, every year we allocated more resources to the schools budget than central government targets suggested.

Improvement of the school system was not just achieved by allocating more resources from the centre. We also encouraged our councillors to be involved as governors of local schools. I remember an incident at a governors' meeting in Westfields School, in the heart of Mortlake ward, which epitomised the difference between the Labour Party of the 1980s and us. The head teacher organised regular visits from the governors, and at the regular governors' meeting a nominee of the Labour Party complained that during her regular visit she had noticed that the girls were asked to run errands and the boys to move furniture. This was not politically correct.

The poor head teacher struggled to find an answer to satisfy our colleague and we moved on. I thought no more about this until a year or two later when I read in the local paper that the lady in question and her husband, a well-known lawyer, had been accused of illegally over-working their au pair girl. The difference between Labour Party theory and practice, I thought.

Third, we were at the forefront of the recycling revolution. When we had been in opposition we had used volunteers on the fourth Sunday of the month to collect used newspapers from households who signed up to the scheme and take them for disposal to a bus depot in the centre of Richmond owned by a local councillor. This provided revenue for the constituency association, although this dwindled as the price for used newsprint dropped. When we took control of the council we introduced a council-run recycling scheme, which is of course now ubiquitous throughout the United Kingdom.

Fourth, we were among the first to introduce employment practices that ruled out discrimination on grounds of race, gender or sexual orientation. In the early 1980s few political figures had come out as gay, so when I was invited to explain our policy to a gay rights fringe meeting at the party conference in Blackpool I was surprised to see so many colleagues in the audience whom I knew well without having realised they were gay.

We certainly learnt how to be a party of government rather than opposition. I used to give talks to Liberal groups who were challenging to take control of a council. I had six rules:

Rule One:

Civil servants hate change; that is why they are civil servants. *Yes Minister* is not a joke. It is a paradigm of civil servants' behaviour. Their job is to ensure the efficient management by you of the status quo. Your job is to ensure the efficient management by them of the changes you were elected to effect.

Rule Two:

Civil servants are your best councillors. Get them on your side and they can work miracles for you. After all, they work at City Hall full time, have control of budgets and can solve all your casework problems if they choose to.

Rule Three:

Most Tories are not at all nice. To paraphrase John Stuart Mill, not all Tories are nasty but most nasty people are Tories. Don't be seduced into consensus by the siren voices of apparently reasonable Tory councillors. Remember that the Tory councillor with the broad hat and ready smile who is kind to dogs and children usually believes that council tenants still keep coal in the bath and that castration is too lenient a punishment for gays.

Rule Four:

Labour can be worse. Labour councillors are more insidiously dangerous because they tend to be nicer. Be particularly on your guard against Labour councillors who come, like the Greeks, bearing political gifts. The Labour leader ultimately wants only one thing – your job.

Rule Five:

It's a team game. It really is like football. Although the star leader can score the occasional flashy goal, you can stay on top of the league only by team effort. So don't appear to take decisions alone, nurture your committee chairs and don't neglect your group. Apart from anything else, they elected you – and can replace you.

Rule Six:

Use your patronage. The biggest gift you have is the power of patronage – use it. First, make sure everyone in your team has some responsibility and title – however meagre. In politics, idle hands make for conspirators. Second, make sure you entrench your supporters en masse in outside organisations. You will lose power at some stage. Make sure that like-minded people are left in positions that will survive you.

I wrote this in 1985. I wonder how much is relevant today to the coalition government.

Looking back to those years as deputy leader, I have a kaleidoscope of memories. We were never immune from central government influence, not always benign. But I certainly felt we scored a point against Nicholas Ridley, Secretary of State for what was then called the Department of the Environment. He rang me one day to say that he wanted to appoint our chief executive, Michael Honey, as chief executive of the London Docklands Corporation. The problem was that he was either on three or six months' notice and they wanted him to start quickly. Would we release him from his notice period? I discussed this with David Williams and we agreed we should ask for a quid pro quo. The government had introduced a system of controls on councils spending their receipts from the sale of council assets. We were planning a redevelopment of a site in Twickenham, so I asked the Secretary of State if the capital receipt could be outside the controls. He agreed, so we agreed to release our chief executive from his notice period. I doubt if that would happen today.

The highlight of our redevelopment of council-owned properties was undoubtedly our scheme to renovate a site on the River Thames next to Richmond Bridge, partially owned by the council and partially by a property developer. When we took control of the council in 1983 we vetoed the plans on the table and persuaded the developer to produce a higher-quality scheme on such a prestigious site. The developer introduced a scheme by Quinlan Terry, the pastiche architect so loved by Prince Charles.

So high-profile was the scheme that the Queen came to open it. The Queen came by river and frogmen had to search the river banks for bombs before her arrival. It was a sunny day, so the council hierarchy lined up on the river bank to be presented and then went inside for drinks and canapés. Was it the effect of the wine or did I dream the conversation I had with Quinlan Terry when I congratulated him on his design? All I know is that I asked him about his motivation to become an architect and in reply he said I obviously did not know that Moses had appeared to him and presented him with his architectural instructions. When I showed surprise, he told me that everyone looked at him like that when he told them the story.

Notwithstanding government financial pressures, we were anxious to promote the arts in the borough. The

Orange Tree Theatre in the centre of Richmond, above
a pub, deserved and received council funding. But the
Richmond Theatre on Richmond Green was facing financial difficulties. The theatre was bought by Sally Greene,
a dynamic and attractive woman who later went on to
great success with the Old Vic. David Williams and I had
instituted a system of weekly meetings in the town hall in
Twickenham with the chief executive, Michael Honey, and
the finance director, Richard Harbord. We met in the early
morning and I used to take the train from Barnes to Twickenham and then to my office in London. At one of our
meetings Michael Honey dropped in a comment that he had
recently had lunch with Sally Greene and thought we should
give a council guarantee to underpin the redevelopment of
the theatre. David and I were not persuaded and I said that
I felt her wealthy property developer husband was a better
bet than us. A few weeks later, Sally Greene invited me to
lunch at the Groucho Club and tried to use her legendary
charm on me. The lunch was good and she was charming
but I stuck to my guns. To my amazement, a few weeks later
the director of finance told me that he had committed us to
the guarantee. He confirmed that Sally Greene had taken
him to lunch. No wonder she was able to persuade Kevin
Spacey to come and run the Old Vic years later! Effectively,
the council took over the financing of the theatre, in a transaction the council has only recently paid off.

Although I stood down from the council in 1998 and have played no direct role in Richmond politics since then, the past still comes back to haunt me from time to time. There are still people who believe that I closed Richmond ice rink, although it was not a council facility and was closed by its property company owners. Recent allegations of sexual abuse by Cyril Smith, the former Liberal Member of Parliament for Rochdale, provoked a serious libel of me on a blog by David Hencke, an investigative journalist who had retired from *The Guardian* newspaper. Apparently, I had covered up Cyril Smith's activities at a children's home in Barnes. I had in fact never met Cyril Smith and was not aware of the allegations against him until they were aired in a television programme made in 2013. In any event, the children's home in question had closed in 1982, the year before we took control of the council. This sort of publicity is always personally distressing. I could have sued David Hencke. There can be no more serious libel than an allegation that someone covered up sexual abuse by a political colleague. I decided that time and effort, let alone finance, made a libel action not worthwhile, but I would sue if the allegation ever appeared in print. So far it has not, but my dilemma is an example of the problems created by the internet. Alistair McAlpine decided to sue anyone who had suggested on the internet that he was a paedophile and gave the money to charity. Hopefully this gave pause to those who felt they were libel-free for any accusation, however outrageous.

A more amusing incident occurred when I was in a small art gallery in Shoreditch and found myself talking to a woman whom I had just witnessed handing over a large cheque to the owner for three paintings she had just bought. She told me that she owned a restaurant in Mortlake High Street. When I told her that I must have been her local councillor when she started the restaurant, she said that I couldn't be, as the councillor was that fellow Razzall who had caused her all the difficulties over planning. When I told her that Razzall was me, her face was a picture. I vaguely remembered a concern over parking in neighbouring streets when she opened in 1985. She assured me that she would not stop the cheque, even though the owner was a friend of mine.

For my first ten years as a councillor, my political life was primarily devoted to my local role. National politics intervened from time to time as we could not entirely insulate ourselves from the difficulties the party faced in the 1970s.

We fought a by-election in Barnes at the height of the Jeremy Thorpe scandal, when he was on trial at the Old Bailey following the killing of Norman Scott's dog. We lost by one vote. Unusually, we were able to challenge the result successfully in the High Court, but had it not been for the adverse publicity arising from the Thorpe case we would no doubt have won easily. There was some local unease as people did not realise that the ballot was not totally secret, as with a court order the ballot boxes could be opened to match the electoral number with the ballot paper and discover how the constituent had voted. The challenge was made because a supporter reported that her next-door neighbours had voted in the election and, as Germans, were probably not entitled to be on the register to vote. Our supporter thought they had probably voted Tory.

In the event, several ballots that had been disqualified by the returning officer were counted for us, as the judge felt they had shown a clear intention to vote for our candidate, David Cornwell, who was declared the winner.

In fact, litigation was always part of our armoury, as when we challenged a result in the Whitton ward on the Twickenham side of the Thames. But we were the victims of a judicial challenge ourselves following the election of Adrian Slade to the Greater London Council in 1981 by 115 votes. Edward Leigh, the losing Tory candidate, who went on to be elected Member of Parliament for Gainsborough in Lincolnshire in 1983, challenged the result, fundamentally on the basis that Adrian had exceeded spending limits in the election.

An election court was established, presided over by an

experienced barrister, which met in the council chamber in the town hall in Twickenham. Fortunately, Adrian was not disqualified, although the hearing was highly stressful. He led the Liberal group on the Greater London Council until the council was abolished by the Tory government in 1986 and became the last president of the Liberal Party before the merger with the SDP.

An intriguing aftermath of the court case was a theatrical evening at the Drury Lane Theatre to raise money for Adrian's legal costs. Presided over by David Frost, the performers included many from Adrian's time in the Cambridge University Footlights, including Peter Cook, for whom Adrian is credited with creating the celebrated Mr Wisty character.

The formation of the SDP in 1981 and the creation of the Liberal–SDP Alliance clearly impacted our local activities. When it was decided that we would fight the 1982 London borough elections as the Alliance, I was involved in the negotiations with the SDP to determine the number of seats each party would fight. The negotiations were not difficult, for two main reasons. First, by then the Liberal Party in the borough had built up a successful organisation, so most people who wanted to be politically involved and were anti-Tory and anti-Labour had a successful Liberal Party to join. Second, we were in the heady early days of the Alliance when nothing seemed impossible, so it was easy to persuade the SDP negotiators that they should be allocated seats to fight that privately we felt were unlikely to be won. I was struck in our discussions over a pub by East Twickenham station by the extraordinary optimism of the SDP negotiators – they were going to 'break the mould of British politics' – and their political naivety.

In the event, out of the twenty-six seats we won in 1982 the overwhelming majority were Liberals, although a number of SDP victors were welcome to our group, including Serge Lourie, who had left the Labour Party for the SDP and who many years later became the Liberal Democrat leader of the council.

In 1981 I had a peripheral role in the decision to choose Bill Pitt to fight the Croydon North West by-election. In the first by-election after the creation of the SDP, Roy Jenkins had fought Warrington with Liberal support and narrowly failed to win. The hierarchy of both parties felt that Shirley Williams should fight Croydon North West, but the activists of the London Liberal Party felt otherwise.

I was asked to attend a meeting in a fellow councillor's house in Mortlake, where a group of London councillors had agreed that Bill Pitt must be the candidate. He had fought the seat before, was well entrenched locally and, in any event, after Warrington it was the Liberal Party's turn to fight a winnable by-election. Our view prevailed and Bill Pitt won the seat. This was where the word 'alliance' crept

into the literature, and it subsequently became the name
under which elections were fought until the merger of the
two parties after the 1987 general election. At a dinner in
the Houses of Parliament thirty years later, Bill Pitt's agent
reminded me that I had helped him complete his spending return to stay within the statutory limit – an onerous
task before the limits for by-election spending were raised
substantially some years later.

Encouraged, I suppose, by the prospects of electoral
success for the Alliance in the early 1980s, I did toy with
the prospect of standing for the House of Commons.
I realised that as an active local councillor, which I wished
to continue to be, and a busy corporate lawyer, I could
only really stand in Richmond.

After Stanley Rundle had been forced by ill health to
stand down as the parliamentary candidate immediately
before the October 1974 election, the constituency executive had chosen Alan Watson to fight the seat. Alan was a
well-known broadcaster who had presented *The Money
Programme* and *Panorama* for the BBC. I was asked to
be his agent and we fought a strong campaign against the
sitting Tory, Sir Anthony Royle, but failed to win, notwithstanding a flying visit by helicopter from Jeremy Thorpe.
Alan Watson fought the seat again in 1979 and lost once
more to Sir Anthony Royle, but in 1983 he was faced by a
new Tory candidate, Jeremy Hanley, the son of the wartime

comedian Jimmy Hanley and the actress Dinah Sheridan. Alan lost by only seventy-four votes, but by now he had fought the seat three times without winning.

I was approached by a number of colleagues who encouraged me to put my name forward for the next election. Apart from the fact that Alan had lost three times, some people were complaining that he had taken a job in Brussels after the 1979 election as head of the media operation of the European Commission. They felt that he had not been able to spend enough time in Richmond and had he been in Richmond full time he would have won. Conversely, a number of people felt that as he had lost by only seventy-four votes he had been unlucky and deserved another chance.

Under Liberal Party rules at the time, if a constituency executive voted by a two-thirds majority to readopt the candidate who had fought the previous election, the candidate was readopted without a ballot of the membership. At the executive committee meeting Alan was readopted with the relevant two-thirds majority, so my chance was gone. Although neither of us made it to the House of Commons, we both eventually made it to Parliament, Alan as Lord Watson of Richmond and me as Lord Razzall of Mortlake.

—CHAPTER EIGHT—

PARTY TREASURER

MY REAL START in national politics occurred after our overwhelming triumph in the 1986 local elections. I was approached to stand for national party committees. As I was thought to have some knowledge of finance, I was elected to the party's finance committee. For some reason there were two joint treasurers: Anthony Jacobs, who had made a fortune establishing the British School of Motoring, and Hugh Jones, an ex-diplomat who had recently stood down as the party's general secretary. In 1987 they made it clear that they would be happy to stand down if suitable replacements could be found.

I drove down to Guildford one Saturday morning to see Chris Fox, who had just returned from an overseas posting with one of the major firms of chartered accountants. I persuaded him to stand with me and we were duly elected as joint treasurers, with Chris taking responsibility for the party's budgets and me taking responsibility for national party fundraising.

The party leadership had been badly scarred by the Jeremy Thorpe saga ten years previously, where, apart from the trial at the Old Bailey, Jeremy Thorpe had been seriously criticised internally for siphoning donations into an account he controlled, ostensibly to be spent in winnable seats. David Steel, who had succeeded Jeremy Thorpe as leader, made it clear to me that he really did not want much involvement in asking people for money. That was my job. I was on my own.

I had limited success in my two years as Liberal Party treasurer. Indeed, I was the last ever treasurer of the Liberal Party, as in 1988 the party merged with the SDP and the Social and Liberal Democrat Party was created, now known as the Liberal Democrats, and the Liberal Party ceased to exist.

The months leading up to the merger were fraught for both parties. I was invited as a guest to the SDP conference in Sheffield, where the resolution was to be put to approve the merger with the Liberal Party. So I witnessed at first hand the chaos when an attempt was made to prevent David Owen holding a separate meeting to oppose the merger.

I managed to sneak into the David Owen meeting and was stunned by the expressions of rapt adoration on the faces of the audience – particularly the women – and understood for the first time his magnetic appeal.

David Owen made it clear that if the merger proceeded he would maintain a separate SDP, and was followed by a significant minority of the party. The majority felt, with some justification, that the man who had left the Labour Party primarily on the issue of 'one member, one vote' should have respected the democratic wishes of the majority of the SDP.

Although the problems of the Liberal Party were not as acute as those of the SDP, there were undoubtedly issues. A number of leading Liberals were declining to join the merged party and the finances were potentially a mess. It was naively assumed that the membership income of the merged party could be calculated by adding the SDP members who had voted for the merger to the Liberal Party membership, with some allowance for drop-off. This proved to be a gross miscalculation. The major problem was that the Liberal Party did not have a centralised membership system, so the estimates of gross constituency membership were wildly overstated. In addition,

fewer SDP members than anticipated signed up to the
merged party.

In the run-up to the merger, a working party from
both parties was established to plan finances and I found
myself the Liberal Party representative, as my fellow treasurer, Chris Fox, was not in favour of the merger. My SDP
counterpart was Ian Wrigglesworth, now Lord Wrigglesworth, who became a close friend. Ian had left the Labour
Party for the SDP in 1981 and had held his parliamentary
seat in Stockton in 1983, losing in 1987. Ian told me at the
time that until he started to deal more widely with Liberal members and activists he had believed that we were
all bearded, sandal-wearing nutters. When I asked him
how he formed that view, he told me it was derived from
the remarks made to him by the Liberal Party parliamentary leadership.

Before we could start to implement the merger, we had
to elect the officers of the new party. An acting national
executive had been established, with equal SDP and Liberal membership. Ian Wrigglesworth assured me that the
SDP members would support me for treasurer, so I turned
up for the executive meeting in the wood-panelled board-
room in Cowley Street. No. 4 Cowley Street had been the
headquarters of the SDP and was to be the headquarters
for the Liberal Democrats for the next fourteen years.

When the election of a treasurer was reached on the

agenda, my name was proposed and, much to Ian Wrigglesworth's surprise, so was Clive Lindley's. Clive was a Welsh businessman who was close to Roy Jenkins. I remember Ian walking round the table and whispering to various of his SDP colleagues that they should vote for me. As the result of his intervention, I won. Ian went on to be elected by the membership as the first president of the new party, is now in the House of Lords and, ironically, today holds the post of party treasurer that he fixed for me all those years ago.

So began twelve years as party treasurer, with overall responsibility for all party funding. Clearly, the priority was to raise money for general elections, where we were always outspent by the other two parties, as indeed we were in the 1997 election by Jimmy Goldsmith's Referendum Party, which spent £20 million of his money and failed to win a seat.

I was given considerable assistance by Leonard Smith, who had raised significant sums for the party previously and was now a pillar of the National Liberal Club. He sat me down in the club one afternoon and gave me a potted history of the lives and foibles of countless potential donors, with anecdotes that were often defamatory and which I had better not repeat.

I quickly learnt that there are only three ways to ask for money for a political party. You can write to, meet or telephone a possible donor. You are also subject to the 80/20 or even 90/10 rule: 80 to 90 per cent of your money will come from 10 to 20 per cent of your supporters. So a mass mailing campaign will be effective with the 80–90 per cent and bring in 10–20 per cent of the money. Mass mailing requires an organisation, which we set up at party headquarters. The big donors were for me to meet and schmooze with the help of Paddy Ashdown, who had been elected leader in 1988 and took a totally different approach from David Steel with regard to the involvement of the leader in the fundraising effort.

The early days were more notable for our failures than our successes. Charles Forte, then Lord Forte, had invited Paddy to lunch at the Trust House Forte Headquarters, so Paddy took me with him. We went up in the lift to the dining room on the top floor and did not know what to expect. Charles Forte had by then handed over the running of his business to his son Rocco, but was clearly still involved, as he kept asking the butler when his son would be there. At the end of the lunch he gave me a cheque for £5,000 and told me to write to him every six months or so and he would give a repeat donation. Paddy and I left very pleased with ourselves. When I wrote six months later as requested, I received a reply that he did not understand why I was writing to him as he had always been a Tory!

Michael Ashcroft was another who approached us.

Again, Paddy was invited to lunch at Michael Ashcroft's company headquarters and took me with him. Michael Ashcroft sat opposite us across the lunch table with two colleagues and fired a number of questions as to why we thought he should support the Liberal Democrats. He and his colleagues sat on one side of the table with us opposite and it was as if we were being interviewed. We did not think the lunch went well and so I was not surprised to hear that he had later become a big supporter of the Tories and is now Lord Ashcroft, a Tory peer. I assume that he had decided he wanted a political role and was interviewing different political parties. I wonder how the Labour Party fared.

The Rothschild family donation came to an end on my watch. I had been advised to write to Dolly Rothschild every Christmas and for the first two or three years received a generous donation by return. She was the widow of a Rothschild who had been elected as a Liberal Member of Parliament in the 1929 general election. Dolly lived in Waddesdon in a substantial country house. I failed to read her obituary (memo to fundraisers: always read the obituaries) and wrote my annual letter. I was sad to receive the reply from Jacob Rothschild, her nephew, the successful financier who had inherited Waddesdon, to the effect that the family were not Liberal Democrats and could I possibly desist from further begging letters.

Lord Rothermere, the proprietor of the *Daily Mail*, was another possibility. Chris Huhne, then a Member of the European Parliament, organised a City dinner to raise money and support. I was surprised to find myself placed next to Jonathan Rothermere, clearly with a view to enlisting his support. During dinner I tried my best. Was he pro-European? Yes. Would he give us financial support? No. Why not? The usual response: that he had to be non-political. Final question. As you are so pro-European, how do you let the *Daily Mail*, which you own, be so anti-European? Because my father taught me that I should always trust my editor.

Mohamed Al Fayed was another prospective donor to whom we came close.

Mohamed Al Fayed had first come into my life when he bought the Dorchester Hotel – or so we thought.

My law firm had represented an American group who had acquired the Dorchester Hotel the previous year. After several approaches from Mohamed they agreed to sell for a price that would realise them a huge profit. The negotiations were relatively straightforward except for the presence at every meeting of a military-looking gentleman who had no obvious role and said nothing. Completion of the transaction was to take place in Paris and all involved travelled in Mohamed's private plane. After take-off my colleague asked if it would be in order if he smoked. Mohamed said he did not permit smoking on his plane, at which point the military-looking gentleman looked across and said, 'Take no notice of him. Smoke if you want to.'

All was revealed on arrival in Paris. My colleague received a call from our Californian clients to explain that following completion it would be announced that the Sultan of Brunei was buying the Dorchester Hotel. Mohamed was simply fronting the transaction. The military gentleman had been sent by the Sultan to ensure that no skulduggery or dishonesty took place in the negotiations.

Mohamed crossed my path again in 1995 when I was raising funds to fight the next election. My colleagues Anthony Lester and Alex Carlile reported that, surprisingly, Mohamed wanted to make a large donation to the party. Alex and I went to see him in his office at Harrods. We went up in the lift to an office with an opulent feel. Now, when you first meet Mohamed, it comes as a shock to realise that although he speaks good English he only uses one adjective – the f word – and he uses it every third or fourth word.

'So Mohmmed, why do you want to support the Liberal Democrats?'

'Because I hate the f****** Tories and particularly that f***** Michael Howard.'

Why he hated Michael Howard so much was not clear. He said it was to do with some Welsh secondary bank scandal but I suspect it was because he blamed Michael Howard for his being refused a British passport.

In any event, we discussed a donation of £1 million – a huge amount for us. We had decided that although disclosure of donors was not required at that time, the donation would leak, so he would have to issue a press release that he was now supporting the Liberal Democrats and was making a large donation to the party. We would draft the press release, so we left saying we would clear the procedure and get back to him. Alex said he needed to buy a dinner jacket and Mohamed told him to take anything he wanted. Alex wisely refused the offer.

At our conference in Glasgow shortly afterwards, I briefed Paddy Ashdown and other party officers about Mohamed's offer. After considerable discussion Paddy said we shouldn't do it. At the time as party treasurer I was a bit miffed, but on reflection Paddy was probably right. Whether we would have got the money, who knows?

Some years later I bumped into George Carman, who was representing Mohamed in the Neil Hamilton libel case. 'Are you putting Mohamed in the witness box?' I asked.

'I'm going to have to,' he said.

'What are you going to do about the problem?' I asked.

George immediately knew that what I meant.

'I am arranging for elocution lessons,' he said. I think the appearance in the witness box was satisfactory.

Whether the elocution lessons provided a permanent solution, I do not know. I haven't seen Mohamed since.

Alan Coren was another whose arm I tried to twist.

I had long admired Alan, first as editor of *Punch* and then as a fabled columnist for *The Times* newspaper. I met him through his son Giles, who had been at school and university with my daughter and then lived with her for a number of years when they were in their twenties. As prospective, but never actual, fathers-in-law, our paths often crossed. During our children's romance he was living in the Cricklewood he had immortalised in numerous novels, where I from time to time found myself at lunch or dinner, as I tried to extract a political donation. I suspect Alan was a closet Tory so I had no success.

Many people who are witty on screen or in print are often dull or depressive in real life. This was not true of Alan. He was the funniest man I ever met. Giles and Victoria Coren have published a collection of his work, but so many anecdotes stay in the memory. One time he was asked about internet wars and replied that the only war he knew about was when you were handed a rifle and told to shoot anyone who put a verb at the end of a sentence. Or the wonderful occasion described by Sandi Toksvig at his memorial service. Alan and Sandi had been asked by the editor of *Call My Bluff* to entertain the singer Cliff Richard in the green room. Neither of them knew what to say to him, so Sandi opened with a polite 'I like your tie, Sir Cliff.'

'Thank you,' came the reply. 'It's a Galtieri.'

'That's interesting,' says Alan, 'I always wondered what he did after the Falklands War.' There was no further conversation possible.

John Cleese was what football pundits might call a score draw. John had been an SDP supporter from the early days and had made what was an iconic party election broadcast for the SDP in the 1987 election. When I first met him he was a household name thanks to his roles in *Monty Python* and *Fawlty Towers*. Paddy Ashdown had invited him to attend one of our conferences after I became treasurer and suggested I should ask him for a significant donation, as he had just sold his video training business.

I took him for a drink and his explanation as to why this would not be possible was straight from Basil Fawlty. He agreed that he had received a substantial sum. However, he explained that he could not give me a donation as he had to deduct all the liabilities to be met from the money he had received. Indeed, at one stage I thought he would ask me for a loan.

Although that meeting produced no significant donation, John remained supportive to the party, particularly to Paddy Ashdown. Indeed, he has disclosed that he turned down an offer by Paddy to nominate him as a life peer, saying that the time commitment would be too great.

Even after Paddy's resignation, his support continued. He narrated a party radio broadcast in the 2001 election and tweeted his support for Nick Clegg in 2010. So our courting of John was certainly not a waste of time.

Of course, until the late 1990s all political donations could be kept secret, although pressure to require disclosure was mounting. Andrew Neil used to present a late-night political TV programme, *The Midnight Hour*, where I was often asked to appear as a Liberal Democrat on Thursday nights, as Members of Parliament had usually left London to return to their constituencies. I was somewhat surprised one Thursday night when the Tory MP James Gray defended lack of transparency on the basis that the Tory Party vetted their donors so that was OK. Tory vetting of Asil Nadir before disclosure was required, and our subsequent vetting of Michael Brown after transparency was introduced demonstrated that no vetting system can eliminate inadvisable donations.

The secrecy of donations also meant that people could give money to more than one political party. This was certainly so in the case of an Indian billionaire who phoned my office asking to speak to Jack Cunningham, now Lord Cunningham, my Labour Party counterpart. As his donation was secret I should not name him, but I was amazed to arrive at his office to be given a suitcase containing £50,000 in cash. Now, it is difficult to pay that amount of cash into a bank account without explaining where the money came from, which I had promised not to do.

Ladbrokes came to my rescue. As is so often the case, bookmakers get the odds wrong for some political betting and they were giving good odds on some Liberal Democrat seats that I felt confident we would win. So I placed the money on four Liberal Democrat candidates on the basis that the party would keep any profit and I would underwrite any loss. We made a profit!

Not all of our approaches to the great and good ended in failure. Lack of transparency and the absence of any restriction on overseas donations gave me a huge opportunity in the run-up to the handover of Hong Kong. Paddy Ashdown, along with Mark Bonham Carter, had taken up the cause of UK passports for Hong Kong residents who were nervous of the forthcoming Chinese takeover, so we were well placed to receive a warm welcome there. Paddy also knew Hong Kong well, as he had been stationed there in his military days during the Cultural Revolution when there was fear that the Chinese might invade. But the main architect of our fundraising success in Hong Kong was Sir Michael Sandberg, who had recently retired as chairman of the Hong Kong and Shanghai Banking Corporation.

Michael was still hugely respected in the Hong Kong

community, particularly among Chinese multimillionaires, many of whom owed their fortunes to funding from Hong Kong and Shanghai Bank, now of course HSBC, probably the largest bank in the world. Although now sadly ailing in health, he was then a life force, always greeting me by asking whether we were going dancing. He had started in the army in India, joined the bank there and worked his way to the top in Hong Kong. I understand that before Michael, white bankers did not deal with Chinese customers, leaving it to Chinese intermediaries. Michael changed all that and set the bank on the path of growth from a small Hong Kong bank to the giant it is today. Michael was obsessed with all sports, had been chairman of the Hong Kong Jockey Club and, like his father and grandfather before him, chairman of Surrey County Cricket Club. The large clock with moving cricketers outside the pavilion at the Oval cricket ground was conceived and donated by Michael.

The esteem in which Michael is held in Hong Kong was demonstrated one day over lunch with Li Ka Shing, our host, known ubiquitously as KS, who was by then one of the richest men in the world. Michael had provided him with funding through the Hong Kong and Shanghai Bank in his early days and the Bank's growth had been very much in parallel with the growth of KS's businesses.

Michael told me that when he first met KS, who came to borrow money to acquire some land to develop port facilities, the latter said he could not offer security but could offer his word on the repayment terms. So Michael authorised the loan.

Paddy Ashdown and I were invited with Michael to the private dining room at the top of the KS office building in Hong Kong. There were five or six of us sitting around a table and standing behind us against the wall on each side of the room were five or six uniformed waiters.

In the middle of the conversation Michael turned to our host and said, 'Don't be so bloody stupid, KS.' I saw the waiters opposite flinch and start forward then stop. Clearly, no one spoke like that to KS without being ejected. But Michael could.

We raised significant sums from Michael's contacts in Hong Kong, reassuring them that their identities as donors would not be disclosed. After our first visit I was amused to read a *Sunday Telegraph* article listing Hong Kong donors who were supporting the Tory Party. All those listed had given money to me. So, on our next trip we were able to obtain a second donation from a number of them, as it was clear that even if the Tories leaked their names we did not.

On one of our trips Michael managed a trick I have never seen performed before or since. He had booked a private dining room at the top of the Peninsular Hotel and invited eight wealthy contacts for dinner. The Chinese

food was mouth-watering, the wine flowed and the atmosphere was convivial. At the end of dinner he asked Paddy
and Jane Ashdown to leave and told the table that he and
Tim Razzall had business with them. He stood up, locked
the door and told the assembled company that he was tired,
didn't have long, but wasn't opening the door until everyone committed to send a cheque for at least five or six
figures to me at my hotel the next morning. They agreed.
We left. The cheques all came by 11 a.m.

Of course, our visits to Hong Kong were not purely to
raise money. Chris Patten was by then Governor and Paddy
had a number of conversations with him about the passport issue and the handover scheduled for 1997. He even
warned us about one of our prospective donors, whom the
Hong Kong police feared had committed murder. How
he knew we were dealing with this particular individual,
we did not know; presumably our phones were bugged.

We also visited Beijing and obtained an audience
with Li Lanqing, the Chinese Deputy Premier responsible for managing the handover of Hong Kong. He lived
and worked in the wide, lengthy street containing the
mansions of the Chinese hierarchy. We sat in large arm-
chairs with an interpreter behind each chair. In fact, for
the two main protagonists an interpreter was unnecessary.
Paddy spoke Mandarin and the Deputy Premier spoke
English. Indeed, they found each other contradicting the

interpreters and saying that they had not said what had
been translated. Two statements by the Deputy Premier
stuck in my mind. When asked about the introduction of
democracy in China, he countered by saying that over the
next few years, with the mechanisation of agriculture, 100
million people would have to be moved from the countryside to the towns. While this process occurred, democratic
reforms would be impossible. When pressed on whether
the Chinese would impose a Communist system on Hong
Kong, he said that Deng Xiaoping had talked of one nation
and two systems, which was their intention.

The British ambassador invited us to lunch to quiz us
about our meeting and expressed amazement that we had
access to Li Lanqing. We explained Michael Sandberg's
involvement. There were four men in suits and an attractive woman in the party from the embassy and Paddy took
bets on who was the MI6 operative. He was certain it was
the attractive woman. As we now know that before his
involvement in politics he had worked for MI6, he would
obviously have known.

I came away from Beijing with great respect for the Chinese, whatever the imperfections of their record on human
rights, and certainly found an echo in George Osborne's
comment on his visit there as Chancellor of the Excheq-
uer in 2013 that we must stop looking at China as just a
sweatshop on the Yellow River.

David Alliance was another success. David is an Iranian Jew who came to Manchester as an eighteen-year-old. Manchester had of course been the centre of Britain's textile industry, which had virtually disappeared after the war through overseas competition. Over the years, David rescued the industry by building up Coats Viyella and followed that with N. Brown, a mail order company. David had been an early supporter of the SDP, but as he was close to David Owen he had not initially supported the Liberal Democrats when Owen refused to support the merger with the Liberals and formed the rump SDP. I was delighted to be able to bring David Alliance back into the fold when David Owen wound up his party and he has been a loyal and generous supporter of the party, notwithstanding the introduction of donor disclosure requirements. I was honoured to be asked to be one of his two introducers when Charles Kennedy nominated him to the House of Lords.

David is the most generous host at his house in St John's Wood, where at his annual summer party you progress up a lengthy hall with Lowry paintings either side – what better choice for a Manchester industrialist?

One highlight was an evening with David in St John's Wood when he put together a party to meet the Shah of Iran's son, still called the Shah by his attendant acolytes. The Shah, who lives in the United States, was canvassing for a return to Iran as Shah, where he would immediately

introduce a properly democratic system. We were somewhat startled when Michael Heseltine expostulated that
it had taken a thousand years to create our democracy so
how could he possibly hope to copy us in a few years?
Michael Ancram tried to mediate and soften Michael Heseltine's point, but I fear there was no meeting of minds.

Peter Boizot was always a huge supporter. Peter is a
genuine renaissance man. In business he founded Pizza-
Express and was the first person to import Peroni beer
into the United Kingdom. The business was listed and is
now owned by a private equity group who at the time of
writing are looking to sell for a billion pounds.

For years Peter promoted jazz in London, particularly
in his flagship Pizza on the Park. In sport, Peter sponsored the National Hockey League and played hockey
himself well into his seventies. As a permanent resident of
Peterborough, he renovated the station hotel as the Great
Northern, fought two parliamentary elections for the Liberal Party and rescued Peterborough United, the local
football team. He told me that he had not appreciated that
owning a football club meant that the manager thought he
had an open cheque book.

Peter was always financially generous, including making
the Great Northern Hotel available for strategy meetings.
Sadly, Peter now suffers from one of the debilitating illnesses
that affect elderly people.

I should also mention Sir Eddie Kulukundis. Eddie is a larger-than-life character in every sense. A theatrical impresario and funder of British Athletics, he is married to the actress Susan Hampshire. When I knew him he was at least twenty stone. He told me that he and Susan lived opposite Raymond Blanc's famous restaurant the Manoir aux Quat'Saisons outside Oxford. I assumed that he must eat there regularly, but he said he only kept his wine there in the basement.

Eddie was an unusual donor in that he was obsessed with the minutiae of electoral politics. He used to take Chris Rennard, our campaign chief, and I to lunch at Luigi's in Covent Garden, now sadly closed, and quiz us on the psephological detail of each of our target seats before committing to another donation.

Unfortunately, Eddie was the victim of the Lloyds insurance crash and lost considerable sums. But his generosity to the causes he espoused was legion – to the theatre, to the Liberal Democrats and to athletics. At one stage, before proper funding was available, Eddie was financing a number of our top athletes. Roger Black, the 400m runner, has revealed that when he was out of action for two years and earning nothing, it was Eddie who helped him with his mortgage.

Sadly, Eddie is now struck down with dementia, nursed by his wife. This modest man once opined that his luck was that his parents were very wealthy. He certainly knew how to spend that wealth for the public good.

Success was not necessarily always in the fundraising sphere. I was asked to see a young investment banker who had indicated that he wanted to help us. It was assumed he meant financially, so David Laws was sent to see me. It became clear at once that what he wanted to do was work for the party. He explained that he had made significant money in the City and now wanted to move on. I knew that our treasury spokesman in the House of Commons needed a researcher, so someone of David's background would be ideal. I told him that I would talk to headquarters and come back to him shortly. As he was walking out of the door, I realised we had not discussed salary. He told me that he would be happy to be paid whatever we paid researchers.

David went on to head the party's policy department, and to succeed Paddy Ashdown as MP for Yeovil; he is now in the coalition government.

I realised early on that many potential donors in reality wanted to give money for an honour, particularly a peerage. Every party leader I have worked with has told me how shocked they have been about the number of letters they have received from people promising endless support in return for a peerage.

It was the Liberal Prime Minister Lloyd George who

developed the sale of honours for political donations into an art form. He did defend this once on the basis that it is better to sell honours than sell policies, as they do in the United States. With rare exceptions, we have not allowed big money to influence specific policies in the way that so besmirches American politics. But we have made raising money in return for an honour a criminal offence. There cannot be a fundraiser for any political party who does not have to warn potential donors that what they are asking for would constitute a criminal offence.

In the run-up to the 1997 election I was approached by a donor who offered a large donation if he could be made a peer. I explained over lunch that no donation could be linked to a peerage but I was sure Paddy Ashdown would consider him after the election. That wasn't possible. He wanted the peerage now or he wouldn't make the donation. I was a smart lawyer so he was sure I could get round the law. When I told him that this was impossible, he asked me to take him to see Richard Holme, who was running the election campaign. Richard agreed to see him with me provided he didn't talk about a peerage. Five minutes into our tea, he brought it up. Richard gave him the same answer I had, so he left. Richard laughed and said he was just like the double glazing salesman who knocks on your door and when you tell him you are not interested won't go away and keeps trying to sell you double glazing.

Alexander Thynn was a different story. He was already a peer as he had just inherited the title of Marquess of Bath and the Longleat estate in Wiltshire with the famous lions. He asked to see Paddy Ashdown to discuss whether he should take the Liberal Democrat whip and give us financial support. I went to the meeting. Alexander has a reputation with the tabloids as an eccentric, particularly with the stories about his wifelets. I have always found him to have a sharp political brain.

At our first meeting it was clear that he was fundamentally a Liberal Democrat. I suggested that he might come to our September conference as a visitor to test the water. He felt that would be impossible as he always spent the autumn abroad, I think in the south of France. All went well until he stood up to leave, saying he would certainly support us, provided we were in favour of independence for Wessex. Paddy looked stunned and turned to me. I said that our party had always supported devolution of power and regional government in England. That seemed to satisfy him and he took the Liberal Democrat whip in the House of Lords until the hereditary peers were removed in 1999. He has since proved a valuable financial supporter, particularly locally.

There were many who offered us significant donations without any apparent prior connection to the party. Some, with good reasons, felt that they could make a big

contribution in the House of Lords but for whatever reason had not previously been able to involve themselves
in party work. Someone in this category was George Carman QC. George's professional career was linked to the
party, as he had first risen to prominence in successfully
defending Jeremy Thorpe at the Old Bailey. Shortly after
Charles Kennedy succeeded Paddy Ashdown as leader of
the party, he and I were invited to a *Private Eye* anniversary party in, of all places, the National Liberal Club. We
walked in and found ourselves standing at the bar next to
George, who introduced himself. He explained that he had
always been a Liberal Democrat supporter and if it would
be of interest he would love to work for us in the House
of Lords. Charles suggested he call me the next week to
discuss how all this worked. Later, Charles and I agreed
that he would be a huge feather in our cap and a valuable
member of the House. When George phoned me the next
week, I explained how the system worked. The Prime Minister would at some stage tell Charles how many Liberal
Democrat peers Charles could nominate in the next list. At
that time we would come back to George to have further
discussions, if Charles was offered a reasonable number.
George accepted this and when I bumped into him socially
over the next year or two, I repeated what I had told him.
Sadly George died before Charles was offered another list,
on which I am sure he would have been included.

After his death, George's son Dominic wrote a book in which he suggested that George felt betrayed by Charles and me, as we had offered him a peerage and Charles had reneged. That was absolutely not the case, as I have explained, and it was a tragedy that George died when he did.

The link between donations and honours came to a dramatic head with the police investigation of various colleagues of Tony Blair who had allegedly provided loans to the Labour Party in return for offers of peerages. No prosecutions followed but the strain on those being investigated was enormous, not least on Michael Levy, by then Lord Levy.

Michael Levy had crossed paths with me in several ways. I was already treasurer of the party when he started raising money for Tony Blair and from time to time we found ourselves competing to attract support from prospective donors. But my first dealings with Michael had not involved politics.

In the early 1990s, I was combining my legal work with my role as party treasurer. On this occasion I was the lawyer acting for Time Warner, who were negotiating to buy Michael's recording company, Magnet Records. The negotiations were tricky, not least because Michael kept complaining to Ramon Lopez, the Time Warner executive responsible for the deal, that I was being difficult. In fact, I had a back channel to the client's legal department in New York, who kept telling me to stick to my guns. When we came to the crunch meeting in the office in Lincoln's Inn Fields to agree and sign the sale and purchase agreement, I told Ramon Lopez to turn up at 7 p.m., when we should be ready to sign. He came but we were still arguing about a particularly tricky point where Michael's team wished to delete a clause on which I was insisting. At about 9 p.m. Ramon lost patience and produced a novel suggestion.

He asked me what I thought the point was worth. I guessed that it was worth half a million pounds.

He then turned to Michael and suggested he tossed him for it on the basis that if Ramon won the clause it stayed in but if Michael won it was deleted.

The expression on the faces of the money men in suits who had come over from New York was priceless when Michael agreed.

Then our recollections diverge. In my memory, Ramon won; in Michael's, he won. I suspect that reflects our personalities. What is certain is that Time Warner recouped the purchase price in three years from sales of the music of Michael's major artists.

After the deal was completed, Michael invited me to lunch in a flat he had near Harley Street. Over an entertaining couple of hours he asked me a number of questions about how I raised money for the Liberal Party. I wondered at the time whether I should ask him for a donation, but felt it might be unprofessional to do so in the circumstances so close to the completion of the transaction, as I had met him in such a different context.

I was intrigued when, a year or two later, Michael emerged as Tony Blair's major fundraiser. For a time, largely through Michael's success, the proportion of Labour funding coming from individuals rather than the trade unions significantly increased.

The perils of political fundraising were demonstrated by the police investigation of Michael Levy and his colleagues. But we had our own problems, arising from a large donation by Michael Brown in the run-up to the 2005 election. I had stepped down as party treasurer in 2000, but inevitably had dealings with Michael Brown as I was chair of the 2005 general election campaign.

Michael Brown was what the security services would term a walk-in. He contacted Charles Kennedy's office and offered financial help. Anna Werrin, who had been at Charles's side from the time of his election to Parliament in 1983, referred Michael to Reg Clark, who had taken over from me as party treasurer in 2000. Reg was of course aware that Michael was resident in Majorca, but although a donation from an individual resident overseas was not permitted, a donation from a company trading in the United Kingdom owned by that individual was perfectly legal. Michael indicated to Reg that a company trading in the United Kingdom would make a donation, so there seemed no reason why a donation of £150,000 should not be accepted. Michael also had his own plane and offered to make it available to Charles for his trip to Harrogate for the party conference in March.

At the conference in Harrogate I had my first dealings with Michael Brown, as he had indicated to Anna Werrin that he wanted to make a further donation to the forthcoming election campaign. As I was chair of the campaign I needed to meet him to discuss how the money would be spent.

Michael was unusual in various ways. He sported a pigtail, not standard hairstyle for a significant party donor. He had no apparent background or involvement in politics. But, most intriguingly, he didn't seem to want anything. He did not angle, like so many donors, for a knighthood or peerage. He had no interest in influencing party policy. When asked his motivation, he simply replied that he liked Charles Kennedy, felt the Liberal Democrats were not competing on a fair field financially and wanted to rectify our disadvantage. As Charles, Anna and I got to know him better over the next few months we concluded that all he wanted was to be close to Charles. Apart from Anna, Michael clearly was hostile to anyone close to Charles, including me, which, bearing in mind subsequent events, is perhaps fortunate.

He had certain obsessions about how Charles should receive more publicity, particularly in the tabloids. I remember going with Anna to his flat in Dover Street in Mayfair to meet a man he described as a leading member of the paparazzi. We were told that Michael's friend could secure complimentary photos of Charles in the tabloids. We were not convinced and neither was Charles when we told him.

So, shortly before the starting gun was fired for the election campaign, Michael made a donation of just under £3 million through his United Kingdom trading company. Reg Clark had retired as treasurer and it had been decided to wait until after the election to elect his successor, so the management of the donation fell on Charles's office and particularly on Anna Werrin. Although Reg conducted some preliminary checks when the first donation was received, Anna felt she should go further. Once a general election is imminent the Special Branch become responsible for the security of all party leaders, so Anna was already in discussion with the officers responsible for Charles's security, and she was therefore able to obtain an off-the-record search of Michael Brown's affairs. Special Branch in any event were concerned to vet anyone flying Charles, which Michael Brown had agreed to do. The report came back to Anna that the relevant company's bank account was sizeable from what were undoubtedly trading activities. So there seemed no reason not to accept the donation. Anna clearly needed to be careful about disclosing the information from Special Branch, as they would never go on the record to disclose how they could obtain the relevant information.

Had we had the money a year earlier I suppose it would have been put to better use in campaigning in our target seats. All we could do in the time available was pay for a national billboard campaign and more leaflets than we would otherwise have been able to afford.

It came as a shock the next year when Michael Brown was arrested and charged with fraud. After jumping bail, he was convicted in absentia and absconded to the Dominican Republic, where he was tracked down and is now in prison. Fortunately, the Electoral Commission were satisfied that we had complied with our obligations under the relevant legislation, so we were not required to repay the money, which of course had in any event been spent.

The background to the fraud for which Michael Brown was convicted has never been clear to me. Indeed, as he was convicted in absentia I am not clear whether his side of the story was ever given in court. I assume that he was running what is known as a Ponzi scheme, made infamous recently by Bernie Madoff, where new money is used to pay generous returns to previous investors – the famous chain-letter concept. I do know colleagues for whom Michael's business made money, and indeed stood bail for him, presumably losing their money when he absconded.

The lesson for me from the Michael Brown affair is that the rules on party funding require significant reform. This is not a party political dispute. Asil Nadir for the Tories, loans for peerages for Labour, and Michael Brown for us show that unrestricted dependence on private donations invariably leads to scandals, which simply reinforce the public's low opinion of politics. My own view is that the law should be changed to limit any donation to £50,000, with the taxpayer providing matching funding for every pound raised by a party. Special arrangements would need to be made for the trade unions where they are acting as collecting agencies for party members, provided adequate controls are in place to avoid the sort of activities Unite were accused of in Falkirk in 2013, where members were signed up without their knowledge.

An answer to those who argue that taxpayer money should not be used in this way is that taxpayer money is already used to fund opposition parties' parliamentary activity. Without change, more scandals will inevitably occur.

—CHAPTER NINE—

ELECTION POLITICS

ALTHOUGH MY PRIMARY political responsibility after I became party treasurer was to raise money for the party, inevitably I was also sucked into electoral planning.

The 1987 election was the last fought by the Liberals and the SDP as two parties, albeit as 'the Alliance'. In those days the opposition political parties had limited paid staff, so once an election was called a team of volunteers was required at headquarters.

A number of us felt that our election campaign suffered from a lack of 'rapid rebuttal'; when a story broke or a political opponent made a gaffe, we struggled to take it up quickly enough. I was asked to assemble a group of experienced councillors who would listen to and watch the early-morning radio and television programmes and spot either a story or a gaffe. I put together an experienced team, including David Williams and Alison Cornish from Richmond and Graham Tope from Sutton. They phoned me by 8.30 a.m. and I phoned Polly Toynbee with suggestions.

This was my first encounter with Polly, who had fought a parliamentary seat for the SDP unsuccessfully in 1983 and was David Owen's right hand for the 1987 election. I am not sure that many of my suggestions ended up with any comment or action. Polly has of course crossed my path on a number of subsequent occasions, particularly as a political pundit for the *Guardian* newspaper who is now deeply critical of the Liberal Democrat involvement in the coalition government.

I suppose the result of the 1987 election demonstrated conclusively that notwithstanding earlier hopes the SDP were not going to 'break the mould' of British politics. I suspect that there were a number of contributory factors.

The Falklands War in 1982 cannot have helped. Before the Argentinian invasion, Tory fortunes were already beginning to recover, but the success of the military campaign undoubtedly underpinned the Tory success in the 1983 general election. The problems suffered by a third party under the first-past-the-post election system should not be underestimated. In 1983, the Alliance was only 1 per cent behind Labour in the popular vote but won a mere twenty-three seats against the 209 won by the Labour Party. Of the twenty-three Alliance seats won, only six were SDP. For obvious reasons, electoral reform was a key platform for the Liberal Democrats once the merged party was formed, so the loss of the referendum on electoral reform in 2011 was a severe blow. The failure of Tony Benn to become deputy leader of the Labour Party was, with hindsight, also a setback for the SDP, as this would have provided the final evidence that the extreme left had control of the Labour Party and would have precipitated further defections from Labour.

Random chance also played a part. After the Liberal Simon Hughes had won the Southwark and Bermondsey by-election in the run-up to the 1983 election, it was the turn of the SDP to fight the next by-election in Darlington. The chosen candidate was a local television personality, Tony Cook, who proved a disastrous candidate and came third to Labour. It is perfectly possible that had a decent candidate been chosen and won, the Alliance would have won more votes than Labour in the 1983 election, rather than slightly fewer, and would have provoked the destruction of the Labour Party.

But I suspect a major factor contributing to the collapse of early enthusiasm for the SDP was the perception which developed that the SDP was really no different in behaviour from the other parties. The launch of the SDP in 1981 attracted not only defectors from Labour, but a significant influx of members and supporters who had no previous attachment to another party. This group were different from the tired and faction-driven older parties. But, as with all political parties, there were disagreements at the top, and disagreements between members of the so-called 'Gang of Four' began to seep out into the public consciousness. Certainly by 1987 it would not be possible to make the case that the SDP and their allies the Liberal Party were any different from the other parties.

My involvement in election planning became greater once Paddy Ashdown became leader. Paddy had become the first leader of the Liberal Democrats following the merger of the Liberal Party with the SDP in 1988. David Steel, the outgoing Liberal leader, and David Owen, his SDP counterpart, declined to stand. David Owen did not even join the new party, which a majority of his party members had endorsed, but formed the breakaway SDP.

So the two candidates for the leadership were Paddy Ashdown and the longstanding Liberal Democrat MP Alan Beith. Hustings were organised throughout the country for party members to determine the merits of the two candidates. As party treasurer, I was asked to chair each session and finish with a financial appeal to cover the costs of the election. So, as we traversed the country, I had my first exposure to the Ashdown charisma. Although Alan had a far better grasp of party policy, there was no doubt that Paddy would win, which he duly did.

In fact, at that stage I knew Alan better than I knew Paddy. Indeed, on the first fundraising event Paddy attended he called me 'John' throughout. Alan had been an MP for far longer than Paddy, and my Aunt Thora lived in his constituency in Northumberland. I had been particularly impressed with him at the bar at our early '80s party conference in Margate, a town Clement Freud memorably described as 'the departure lounge for life'. I told Alan that my aunt had been very grateful for his help. When he asked her name and I told him, he replied, quick as a flash, that she lived at 10 Bisley Road, Amble. I was seriously impressed and realised how he had held his seat for so long.

At the beginning of Paddy's leadership the continuation of David Owen's rump SDP caused us significant political and financial problems. The first two by-elections of the new parliament saw Steven Norris in Epping and William Hague in Richmond Yorkshire win for the Tories. Had it not been for the rump SDP we would have probably won both, as the combined vote for the Social and Liberal Democrats (as we were then called) and the rump SDP exceeded the winning Tory vote in each case. The

finances of the party were a disaster. The likely membership income for the new party was grossly overestimated
due to the split in the SDP and the absence of an accurate
estimate of Liberal constituency membership numbers.
I had still not been able to launch a significant campaign
for big donors. The party's prospects were not helped by
a dismal showing in the 1989 European election, where
we won no seats and were beaten into fourth place by the
Green Party. At some stage after those elections, polling
showed us, as Paddy put it, with only the margin of error
saving us from no support at all.

But in 1990 things started to improve. After coming
behind the Monster Raving Loony Party in the Bootle
by-election, David Owen decided to wind up the rump
SDP. Then Ian Gow, the Tory MP for Eastbourne and
close confidant of Margaret Thatcher, was assassinated by
the IRA. After some hesitation as to whether we should put
up a candidate in the Eastbourne by-election, we mobilised hundreds of activists to enable David Bellotti to win
this safe Tory seat with a majority of over 4,000.

So we were in better shape by the time of the 1992
election. My involvement in that election was primarily to
raise the money to fund it – which we succeeded in doing.
I was also asked to chair the rallies around the country
where Paddy as leader was the key speaker. These attracted
huge crowds and I was able to wind up with an appeal

for much-needed cash. The rally in St Austell must have attracted over 2,000 people – easily the largest gathering I had ever addressed.

With hindsight, the problem with the 1992 election was that the polls were showing a hung parliament but no one really knew how to deal with this. The decision was taken that this would be raised only in the last week and Dick Newby, who was coordinating the press, was authorised to leak in the last week our proposals for a coalition government. This proved a disaster as the electorate decided that they did not want Neil Kinnock as Prime Minister and did not understand a coalition government. Canvassers reported a strong drift back to the Tories in the last few days among people who had committed to us before the previous weekend. So the result was a Tory victory, with John Major surprisingly returned as Prime Minister.

A highlight of the 1992 election campaign for me was Paddy's appointment of Des Wilson to run the campaign. So Des came back into my life after many years.

To explain, in the school Christmas holidays I used to sell Lyons ice cream at Bertram Mills Circus in Olympia. I shared a fridge with my friend Stewart Smith and we toured the big top with our wares before the show and during the interval. Pay was pretty good for seventeen-year-olds but was subject to a weekly top-up for the fridge who sold the most. Our main competition was from a gangly New

Zealander who introduced himself as Des Wilson. I can't at this stage remember whether he sold more than we did but I certainly can remember the car he sold us. Ten pounds for an old banger – my first car. I took delivery of it at the end of our last day at the circus; Des gave me the keys and left us in the street outside Olympia. Sadly, the car didn't start and Stewart and I pushed it all the way back to my family home in Ealing. Even worse, there was no log book, and no other evidence of ownership could be found, so I suspected that my £10 had bought a car that couldn't start and that Des Wilson probably did not own.

I thought no more about Des until, many years later, he appeared on our television screens as the brains behind the emergence of the homeless charity Shelter. The leopard must have changed his spots, I thought to myself.

I had been aware of his party role in the late 1980s. He became the president of the Liberal Party and was one of Paddy Ashdown's key backers in his campaign for the leadership before being selected by Paddy to run the 1992 election campaign. So, as I was responsible for raising the money to fund the campaign that Des was running, I decided to tackle the car issue head on. 'Des, do you remember that car you sold me thirty years ago? It didn't start and you didn't own it.'

'Are you telling me that they made a bloke party treasurer who was stupid enough to do that?' came the reply.

We repeated that interchange at various public meetings to the amusement of the audience.

Des was a man of huge talents – drive, determination and judgement. But, like all of us, he had flaws – stubbornness, a thin skin and a huge temper. His judgement was shown at its best in the last ten days of the 1992 campaign, when he clearly was not happy with the decision to major on the possibility of a coalition government.

Evidence of his good judgement also came when I reported to him with ten days to go that I had raised more money than budgeted and so he could spend a million pounds more than planned. 'Too late,' he replied. 'We can't spend that effectively in the time available.'

So we ended the 1992 campaign with a financial surplus – unique in the party's history – and valuable in light of our travails in the previous years.

Des Wilson's thin skin had been demonstrated earlier in the year at a meeting of the party's national executive. There has always been a tension between the leader and the relevant party committee as to accountability for the management of the general election. Des took the issue head on, turned up at a single meeting of the executive, had a blazing row with Tom McNally and never appeared again.

Des had a very poor view of Liberal MPs at the time, with one or two exceptions, and privately used to moan that he was spending twenty-four hours a day to get pygmies elected. His view has not changed, as was demonstrated by the article he wrote for the *Mail on Sunday* in April 2014. He explained that his critical view of Liberal MPs came from his experience as party president in 1986, when he first attended meetings of the parliamentary party. He also disclosed that Cyril Smith hated him and wanted to have nothing to do with the 1992 general election campaign. I suppose that in the current climate to have been on the wrong side of Cyril Smith is a badge of honour.

His thin skin and temper sadly ended his relationship with Paddy Ashdown and the party in the run-up to the 1997 election. Some say this was because Paddy wouldn't agree to his terms for running the campaign again, others that he was annoyed that appointments to the House of Lords had not included him. Only Des will know the truth, but harsh words were spoken and he disappeared from political involvement with the party.

An amusing postscript occurred in the build-up to the 1997 election. We were concerned that his anger with Paddy might produce a damaging article or interview. Des was by then working for the British Airports Authority, whose chairman was a friend of David Steel. David phoned his friend to say that it would be unhelpful for the company if Des Wilson was to do this, as the company would be seen to be interfering in the political process. The chairman took the call on his car phone and said, 'I am on loudspeaker and Des is sitting next to me.' In any event, no article appeared.

Looking back, I feel it was all such a pity and even today Des would be a great asset to the party. I learnt a huge amount from him, particularly about crisis management. The major lesson he taught me was that in any crisis, the manager of the media needs to know the whole story so that there are no surprises; all factors must be disclosed straight away, to avoid a steady drip of critical reports giving the story 'legs'. I fear that this lesson has not always been learnt by the Liberal Party leadership, particularly recently, over the allegations against Chris Rennard and Cyril Smith.

The 1992 election had proved a disappointment, as our vote was squeezed through fear of a Labour government. But when John Smith succeeded Neil Kinnock as Labour leader our fortunes started to improve. When support for the Tory government fell off a cliff after the financial crisis known as Black Wednesday in autumn 1992, we were in good shape financially and our opinion poll ratings began to climb. But John Smith's death and his replacement by Tony Blair sucked the oxygen from our rise.

Paddy Ashdown had developed a friendship with Tony Blair before Blair became leader. Indeed, I understand that shortly before John Smith's death Tony Blair had told Paddy over dinner that he felt disillusioned with politics and the future of the Labour Party.

So Blair was to dominate our lives for the next thirteen years. Having developed a friendship with him before he became leader, Paddy continued the relationship through his leadership. It was apparent to both men that there was a constitutional agenda on which the two parties could cooperate, particularly devolution of power in Scotland and Wales.

Others have written in detail about the talks between Robin Cook and Bob Maclennan that formed the basis of the creation of the Scottish Parliament and Welsh Assembly after the 1997 election.

My involvement was on the periphery as a member of the 'Jo Group', which Paddy set up outside any party structure to monitor and advise on his discussions with Tony Blair. It is lost in the mists of time as to whether the group was named after Jo Grimond or Jo Phillips, who worked for Paddy at the time. In any event, the existence of the group was kept secret from the party.

That Tony Blair and Paddy wanted to go further than constitutional reform became clear when, at one of our meetings, Paddy produced a bombshell. Tony Blair would like a coalition with the Liberal Democrats after the election even if Labour won an overall majority. Initially, there was consternation. Did we believe him? How would the party wear it? Would Blair accept a commitment to proportional representation as a condition of the coalition, as we believed that the junior partner in a coalition was most vulnerable at a subsequent election?

The first question was dealt with by a meeting between various colleagues on both sides. It was a lot easier to reach agreement on the issues than to get Donald Dewar to attend. Derry Irvine had been Tony Blair's pupil master when he first went to the bar and was a close adviser. Derry was married to Donald Dewar's ex-wife and Donald eventually agreed to attend the meeting in Derry Irvine's house so long as Derry Irvine did not chair the meeting and Alison Irvine went out.

Apart from these difficulties, the meeting went smoothly. Change to the voting system did not seem to be an issue for the Labour side but the internal party issue was becoming tricky for us as the story was beginning to get out.

It appeared that we would have two or three Cabinet places and it remained to be discussed whether Paddy would stay outside simply as leader of the party.

The run-up to the 1997 election had been promising for the Lib Dems. The opinion polls were consistently poor for the Conservatives. Indeed, Tory support never picked up from a collapse after Black Wednesday shortly after the 1992 election. It was clear that Labour would win the next election. Nevertheless, our by-election victories in Newbury, Christchurch and Eastleigh showed that we could take seats from the Tories if we could demonstrate that the Labour candidate could not win. In 1996 we had tremendous success in the county council elections. I remember being in the Cowley Street headquarters, helping to collate the results and predicting to Paddy Ashdown after an hour or two a projected figure for gains that he simply did not believe. In the end I had underestimated our triumph that evening. As we all celebrated over a drink that night, Lord Tordoff produced a list for Paddy Ashdown of parliamentary candidates who would win their seats in the next year if these results were replicated, many of whom would be regarded as potential troublemakers. Paddy held his head in his hands. As it happened, when the time came none of them was elected.

Paddy Ashdown had asked Richard Holme to chair the 1997 general election campaign. Richard was a totally different kettle of fish from Des Wilson. In business, he had started with Unilever, emigrated to the United States, returned to work for Penguin Books, established a government advisory business and, in the run-up to the 1997 election, was an executive director of Rio Tinto. As one of his daughters memorably said in her speech at his sixtieth birthday party, she always admired her father for his ability to reinvent himself so many times. In politics, he had fought five parliamentary elections, including Cheltenham in 1983 and 1987, but stood down before the seat was won by Nigel Jones in 1992. Suave and debonair, as his obituary later said, he had the looks more of Clark Gable than Errol Flynn.

Richard shared Des Wilson's characteristic of wishing to control every aspect of the campaign. This was a problem in the run-up because of his responsibilities with Rio Tinto, but once he was full time in the role his grip on strategy, tactics and procedures was firm.

Again, as party treasurer I had the responsibility of raising funds for the campaign. But in addition Richard asked me to take on the responsibility for managing the leader's tour. In that election, the aim was to ensure that Paddy Ashdown spent some time in televisual events in as many of our target seats as possible. This required a team to travel the country well in advance to decide locations and to ensure that the local parties would turn out in force on the appointed day. A complex schedule of bus and plane trips had to be planned to take Paddy and the attendant journalists from venue to venue, starting after each morning's press conference. The hard work in advance and during the campaign was performed by a team put together by Sarah Gurling, who later married Charles Kennedy.

The other job Richard asked me to undertake was responsibility for the last week. It was clear that in previous elections our support had peaked on the weekend before polling day and fallen away during the last week

– most noticeably in 1992. So the plan was to increase the level of activity on the ground in our target seats. We also wanted to reinforce the image for television of cheering crowds greeting Paddy Ashdown in a whistle-stop tour of the country. Chris Rennard came up with the idea of large placards to be held by supporters in front of the cameras with slogan such as 'Liberal Democrats winning here'. These are now ubiquitous in Liberal Democrat election campaigns.

We were helped by the fact that most of our target seats were in the south or south-west, so a number could be visited on the same day. Nevertheless, we ran into problems of timing and one day I had to divert the plane that was carrying Paddy to Bridgwater, his next destination. A large crowd had been gathered to greet him in Bridgwater and our candidate, Michael Hoban, claimed that my decision had cost him the election and never spoke to me again. He lost by over 1,700 votes so I suspect I was not to blame.

In the event, notwithstanding the Labour landslide, we won forty-six seats, the best result for us since 1929.

It is clear from *The Ashdown Diaries* that Blair and Paddy confirmed the coalition plans before the election result was known in May 1997. A meeting of the Jo Group was convened in Paddy's office on the Saturday morning after election day, where a call from the new Prime Minister was expected to make the arrangements for the coalition.

Paddy took the call privately and reported back that in light of Labour's overwhelming victory Blair needed a little more time to put things in place and would revert on Monday.

And so this went on for the remainder of Paddy's leadership. The coalition proposal remained on the table for the next two years, followed by constant attempts by both leaders to find ways for the two parties to cooperate. This included the establishment of the joint Cabinet committee to discuss constitutional reform, which hardly ever met, and the appointment of Roy Jenkins to chair a commission on electoral reform. Tony Blair wanted to extend the role of the joint Cabinet committee to go further than constitutional reform. But Paddy insisted that a commitment to electoral reform was essential. So it was Tony Blair's reaction to Roy Jenkins's report that proved the death knell to what had become known as 'the project'. Paddy believed that he had Blair's commitment to implement whatever Roy Jenkins recommended. To ensure this, Roy Jenkins held discussions with Downing Street to confirm that his recommendations would find favour. The closeness of the links with Downing Street was demonstrated by Paddy's office drafting the press release for the Prime Minister to issue welcoming the Jenkins recommendation. But in the end Blair changed his mind, or in any event felt he could not deliver key members of his Cabinet. As reform of the electoral system was a key Liberal Democrat condition for closer cooperation between the parties, although the project limped on it was effectively dead and its failure drove Paddy Ashdown to an early resignation.

The years of Paddy's leadership after the 1992 election had seen triumphs and disappointments in equal measure. The by-election victories in Eastleigh, Newbury and Christchurch, all from the Tories, were sensational, as were the 1996 county council elections. Few forecast the forty-six seats won in the 1997 Blair landslide. But for Paddy the ultimate disappointment was the failure of his attempt with Tony Blair to realign the centre left in British politics. The end of his plans for a coalition government after 1997 and the failure of Tony Blair to implement the recommendation of the Jenkins Commission on electoral reform provoked Paddy's resignation from the leadership of the party in 1999, believing that his political strategy had failed. He did not stand in the 2001 general election. But after his successful four years in charge of Bosnia and Herzegovina, Paddy returned as an active member of the House of Lords, a huge supporter of Nick Clegg and the chairman of the 2015 general election campaign.

My active involvement with him ended with his leadership, and my involvement with his successor, Charles Kennedy, in his absence in Bosnia meant that our lives drifted apart. But my memories of working with him remain vivid.

Paddy is a man of huge energies, whether in insisting on being the first down a black run when the first ski lift starts or thinking nothing of a phone call to an aide at six in the morning. Political parties often elect leaders right for the time and Paddy's energy was essential in pulling the party back from the brink of disaster in the late 1980s. Like all politicians with enormous dynamism, not all of Paddy's initial ideas were sound. As one wag who knew both Paddy and his successor quipped, 'With Paddy you had to spend time persuading him not to do things, with Charles you had to try and persuade him to do something.'

Paddy's ultimate misjudgement, which he would be pleased to have been proved wrong, was to believe that without proportional representation the party would be destroyed once the electorate turned against Labour. In fact, in 2001 and 2005 we increased our number of parliamentary seats and of course in 2010 we held the balance of power and went into government for the first time in peacetime since the 1930s. For all his misjudgement on the likely outcome of a Labour defeat, there can be no doubt that Paddy's leadership allowed us to be regarded as a serious political party and laid the groundwork for the party's position today.

But it is as a friend that I will always remember Paddy. Driving in a procession through a French village to celebrate his daughter's wedding, drinking too much

Glühwein in Val Thorens's highest bar and, amazingly in view of subsequent events, showing him the key towns of Yugoslavia on an atlas before he was interviewed on the *Today* programme.

The 1990s were fun.

—CHAPTER TEN—

THE KENNEDY YEARS

W HEN CHARLES KENNEDY was elected leader
to replace Paddy, I had played a role in his
leadership campaign. For the next seven
years I was one of Charles's close advisers.

I stood down as party treasurer after twelve years and
Charles asked me to become chair of the party's Campaigns and Communication Committee with responsibility
for elections. This was the beginning of my direct involvement with Tony Blair, rather than at one remove through
the Jo Group. Charles felt that the Ashdown project had
run its course but we both saw an electoral opportunity
for cooperation with Labour. We had, after all, had a

surprisingly good result in 1997 and in the overwhelming majority of our held and target seats our main opponent was the Tories. If we could position ourselves with Labour as anti-Tory, electoral dividends should follow. Two against one would benefit us.

Charles and I had several meetings with the Prime Minister and his staff in Downing Street. At the first one we were asked to wait in the Cabinet Room. Charles lit a cigarette, saying, 'I know Tony doesn't like smoking so I want to start by showing our independence.' He was right, so we were quickly ushered into the garden, where the first steps in our electoral cooperation were taken. I remember sitting in the sun in 2000 in the Downing Street garden with Charles, Tony and Anji Hunter, Blair's right-hand woman, and thinking that for a politician, life doesn't get much better than this.

Blair wanted to keep the joint Cabinet committee going and even give it health or education as a joint project. Although Charles resisted these blandishments, Blair was very much up for behind-the-scenes electoral cooperation.

The Prime Minister decided that his old flatmate Charlie Falconer, now a peer, should be the person to liaise with me over election planning. It was Charlie's responsibility to make sure that Gordon Brown, as their election supremo, was kept in the picture. I never spoke to Gordon.

As the 2001 election approached, Charlie and I met

regularly in his spacious room in the Cabinet Office. We were sometimes joined by Douglas Alexander and Pat McFadden. Our tactics were clear. We would concentrate our efforts on seats where our main opposition was the Tories, and Labour would do the same. We recognised that there would be the odd exception, such as Southwark & Bermondsey and Chesterfield, but overall the logic was clear.

In policy terms we would coordinate our attack on the Tories, particularly on the economy, where Labour felt we would be seen as more objective than them. The election campaign itself worked smoothly. Charlie and I spoke every day to ensure coordination of messaging and the two-against-one strategy paid off as Tory fortunes slumped. The one exception was immigration, where our private polling showed a rise in Tory support whenever they majored on immigration, only to fall again when they moved on to other issues.

2001 was the first general election for which I had been responsible as chair of the campaign. Labour had been ahead in the opinion polls and it was generally assumed that Tony Blair would call the election for May 2001, rather than risk the full five-year term to which Labour would have been entitled. In the event, the outbreak of foot-and-mouth disease meant that the election had to take place in June in view of restrictions on movement in the countryside.

Until 2001 our election campaign had required an influx of volunteers into party headquarters, as the party hadn't been able to afford to employ enough paid staff to fill the jobs required by a properly run campaign. This time the situation was different. After 1997 the Labour government had agreed to a significant increase in the so-called 'Short Money', the grant paid to opposition parties designed to improve their capacity to provide effective opposition to the government of the day. This meant we had a much larger team of professional staff available for the general election campaign.

The structure of the campaign was much the same as in 1997. The day started with the leader's press conference, which I had to chair. It was explained to me that when taking questions I should call the broadcasters first in order of seniority – BBC One, ITN, Channel 4, Sky News. The problem was that unless Elinor Goodman was there for Channel 4, all those called first were men. I was somewhat thrown early in the campaign when Jackie Ashley, a political correspondent for *The Guardian*, asked me why I seemed to be calling all men; coincidentally, she is married to Andrew Marr, who was then the political editor of the BBC and whom I tended to call first.

Allegations of sexism followed one day in a less apparent way from our own side. Apart from Charles Kennedy and I, our platform party was varied each day to try to give television exposure to as many candidates as possible. One of our problems was that so many of our candidates in our held or target seas were men, so providing balance was not easy. We gathered in a private room thirty minutes before the start of the press conference to brief Charles and those appearing on the platform on the issues that had emerged overnight and served bacon butties, croissants and tea or coffee. One morning we had asked Jackie Ballard, who was defending her seat in Taunton, to appear with Diana Maddock, the victor of the Christchurch by-election. Jackie took one look at the plate of bacon butties and asked firmly why we were serving such a sexist breakfast. Charles and I were stunned. Diana Maddock looked embarrassed. Jackie lost, but not because of the breakfast!

Contrary to the expectation of most pundits and the pessimists in our ranks, we increased our seats to fifty-two. Labour sources have understandably not focused on their electoral cooperation with us, probably because many of their big beasts had not been told. But Lance Price, Downing Street official, did give the game away at a post-election symposium at Essex University. When asked by Peter Riddell whether Downing Street noticed any difference between Paddy Ashdown and Charles Kennedy as leader of the Liberal Democrats, he memorably replied, 'With Charles we didn't get six faxes a day telling Tony what he should do.'

An amusing personal postscript to the 2001 election occurred when I congratulated Alistair Carmichael on his victory in Orkney & Shetland, where he had replaced Jim Wallace, who was standing down. Alistair told me that on the day before polling day he had been canvassing on a road at the north end of Shetland – probably the most northern road in the United Kingdom.

On knocking on the last door he was asked whether he knew Tim Razzall. 'Well, yes I do.'

'What do you think of him?'

'I don't know him that well, but he's OK.'

'Well, anyone who thinks Tim Razzall is OK is not getting my vote.'

The door was slammed in Alistair's face. I have never been to Shetland, and know no one there. Who it was remains a mystery.

After the election our cooperation continued. Charles had regular meetings with the Prime Minister, much to the irritation of his more 'Old Labour' colleagues. This was illustrated by an encounter with John Prescott in White-hall. At a recent meeting with Tony Blair, Charles had commented on the singing fish in pride of place on the office mantelpiece.

'Oh yes, John Prescott brought it back for me from Florida so I thought I had better put it there.'

'I saw your fish on Tony's mantelpiece,' says Charles.

'Everyone says that,' says John Prescott. 'That's how I keep track of who the fucker is seeing.'

Charles and I agreed with the Prime Minister that we would continue our electoral cooperation against the Tories in the next election. Sally Morgan, who had replaced Anji Hunter as the Prime Minister's political adviser, became my Downing Street contact and we had regular meetings to plot the coordination of our strategy.

Then came the Iraq War. This is not the place to review the Prime Minister's cooperation with George W. Bush in the invasion of Iraq, as others have more internal information than I have. I was surprised that the so-called 'Downing Street memo' written by Matthew Rycroft in July 2002 did not cause greater controversy when leaked to the *Sunday Times* and printed on 1 May 2005 during the election campaign. I had met Matthew Rycroft at the Democrat convention in Los Angeles in 2009 when he was working as a diplomat in our Washington embassy.

By 2002 he was working as the Prime Minister's private secretary, advising on foreign affairs. Matthew's memorandum revealed that President Bush wanted to remove Saddam Hussein by military action, justified by the conjunction of terrorism and weapons of mass destruction. The memo seemed to provide conclusive proof that the decision to remove Saddam Hussein had been taken first

– a clear breach of international law – with the intelligence to support the invasion slanted to that purpose.

Needless to say the Liberal Democrat opposition to the war made our election planning more difficult. But our relationship was helped by Charles's refusal to join the media accusation that the Prime Minister had lied over weapons of mass destruction. Sally told me that his position that the Prime Minister was misguided but not deceitful was appreciated in Downing Street.

So we went into the 2005 election in pretty much the same relationship as in 2001. The two parties positioned themselves two to one against the Tories and for the first two weeks Sally Morgan and I liaised regularly. Apart from our refusal to join in an attack by Tony Blair on the Tory immigration policy, a topic we felt we should keep off, relationships were good. We had decided to save the Iraq War issue for later in the campaign so as not to be seen as a one-trick pony. When we started to raise Iraq after about fifteen days, Sally Morgan complained. I responded that they could not expect us to ignore what was potentially a vote-winning issue for us. But that ended any effective cooperation between us.

We had a slow start to the campaign as Donald Kennedy, Charles and Sarah's son, chose the beginning of the campaign to be born. Menzies Campbell as deputy leader stood in for Charles until Donald was safely delivered and back at home. The structure of the campaign was the same as 2001, with an early-morning press conference to attempt to influence the issues of the day. Charles then spent the day touring the target seats while we dealt with the problems of that day and planned for the next.

Rallies at night attracted huge crowds. I particularly remember chairing a rally in Cambridge, with Menzies Campbell as the warm-up speaker for Charles. Charles was delayed, through the pressure of his itinerary, and I realised I would have to keep the audience entertained until he arrived. After a seventeen-minute impromptu speech I understood how filibusterers in the United States must feel. Fortunately, Charles arrived before I ran out of spontaneous argument.

That was also the night when my briefcase was stolen. Charles and I had similar briefcases and his staff left his next to mine in the green room, available to the speakers for refreshments before the rally. After the rally I picked up the only briefcase left in the green room and went back to London. I assumed that Charles had already taken his. When I opened the briefcase the next morning I realised I had picked up the wrong one. Charles did not have mine, which meant mine had been stolen, despite the fact that the room was guarded by Charles's security officers. Presumably the thief had mistaken mine for his, assuming his contained campaign secrets!

It was a strange election, with the campaigns of the three leaders shortened, not only in Charles's case by Donald's birth, but by the requirement to attend the Pope's funeral and the royal wedding, or, as I memorably described them in a post-election interview, as the Pope's wedding and the royal funeral – the ultimate Freudian slip. But we won sixty-two seats, the largest number since 1929, including fourteen seats from Labour, the first time the party had taken more than one seat from Labour in any election since the creation of the Labour Party.

Inevitably, my relationship with the Prime Minister ended then, as did my role following Charles's resignation in 2006.

It is hard to define a chameleon. For many, Tony Blair was the man who created New Labour and delivered three consecutive election victories – never before achieved by Labour. For others, he was the monster who sent us into an illegal war in Iraq. What were my thoughts on Tony Blair? Did he mislead people? Yes. He clearly misled Paddy Ashdown over both the coalition proposals and reform of the electoral system. Did he do this deliberately? I think not. My view would be that his great strength and his great weakness was a belief that he could persuade anyone to do whatever he wanted. So he underestimated the difficulty of carrying John Prescott and Jack Straw to his vision of linking more formally with

us to destroy the Tory Party. He underestimated the difficulty of carrying Charles Kennedy to share the Paddy
Ashdown vision of 'the project'.

His leadership was made more difficult by his increasingly toxic relationship with Gordon Brown. Plus, his
relationship with parliamentary colleagues was made more
difficult by the command-and-control regime introduced
by Peter Mandelson and Alastair Campbell.

This was demonstrated by the treatment of my friend
Robert Marshall-Andrews, who had been elected as Member for Medway in 1997. I first met Robert when we were
eighteen. I was at St Paul's School, then in Hammersmith,
and he was at Mill Hill, funded by a London county council scholarship.

We played against each other in a First XV rugby game.
Bob likes to tell the story that we sat next to each other
at tea and discussed our futures. We both expressed an
interest in politics. He said he was a Tory and planned to
destroy the Labour Party. I said I was a Liberal and planned
to destroy the Tory Party. So he became a Labour Member of Parliament and, as I write, I am in coalition with
the Tories. Such are the vagaries of political life, although
Tony Blair would say that Bob had a good try at achieving
his teenage ambition.

We met again in the 1960s after university and have
been close friends for nearly fifty years. He was my best

man twice and on the second occasion startled the guests by starting his best man speech with, 'As I was saying…'

During our twenties and thirties we made our way in the law, Bob as a successful barrister and me as a solicitor specialising in corporate law. By the time we were forty Bob had stood unsuccessfully for Parliament as a Labour candidate and I was the deputy leader of Richmond Council. I can remember sitting next to Bob on my fortieth birthday in a restaurant overlooking Notre Dame in Paris and him saying to me, 'If it all ended now, don't you think we have had a great life?'

Little did we know what was to come.

In 1997 Bob was elected as Labour Member for Medway and I entered the House of Lords as a life peer. But Bob did not realise that he had already burn his boats as far as ministerial progress was concerned. Bob is a brilliant after-dinner speaker and in early 1997 was invited to speak at a lawyer's dinner where the chief guest was Derry Irvine, tipped to become Lord Chancellor if Labour won the election. Derry is an outgoing, fun-loving man, partial to a drink or two, if not three. The then Lord Chancellor was Lord Mackay, clever, rather ascetic and probably teetotal. In toasting Derry Irvine, Bob said, 'When Labour wins the election one thing is certain: we will replace one ascetic, teetotal, Scottish Lord Chancellor with another.'

Helena Kennedy, who had chaired the event, rang Bob the next day to tell him he had a problem. Derry Irvine and Tony Blair were upset by his speech and he must apologise. 'Don't be ridiculous,' said Bob. 'It was a joke and I am certainly not apologising.'

When Tony Blair formed his government, Bob was the natural candidate for Solicitor General, as Labour were short of QCs in the Commons. He was passed over. Chris Mullin, chair of the Home Affairs Select Committee, then asked Bob to join the committee. A few days later Chris told him the Whips' Office had vetoed his appointment. Before the summer recess Bob saw the Chief Whip and asked him what the problem was. He was told he was on a Downing Street blacklist because of the speech he had made. So they turned a natural team player into a rebel, who became a thorn in the government's side, particularly on issues of civil liberties and human rights.

The stupidity of the government regarding Bob was demonstrated by an incident several years later, as Bob recalls in his autobiography. He and I were having dinner together in the Peers' Dining Room and Michael Levy, Blair's fundraiser, walked by. I introduced Bob to Michael, who professed not to know who he was. The next day Michael passed me in the corridor. 'You need to be careful of that friend of yours,' he said. 'He's a Trot, you know.'

Nothing could better demonstrate the bunker

mentality that power generates. It was the Labour government that was the loser.

That this bunker mentality continued after the succession passed from Tony Blair to Gordon Brown is demonstrated by the recent revelations by Damian McBride, Brown's press officer, of the calculated briefing against Labour Party colleagues. It would be a pity if Tony Blair is remembered by history only for going to war in Iraq and creating the climate that spawned Damian McBride.

When Charles Kennedy succeeded Paddy Ashdown as leader, most pundits believed that we had reached our high watermark with forty-six seats in the 1997 general election. So to increase our seats to fifty-two in 2001 and sixty-two in 2005 confounded earlier expectations.

On reflection, there were a number of factors that underpinned our steady growth.

First, as I explained earlier, the cooperation with the Labour Party behind the scenes enabled us to focus our resources on the majority of our target seats, where in most cases our major opponent was the Tory Party and the Labour Party was in third place. Two against one in these circumstances produced serious electoral dividends.

Second, the target-seat strategy pioneered in 1997 continued in both elections. With limited resources there was no point in spreading ourselves too thin. So resources from the centre were concentrated on the seats we thought we could win – and mostly did.

Third, we had a close-knit, cohesive team. Until Paddy Ashdown became leader, the management structure for elections was chaotic. Traditionally, the leader appointed an election chair, historically always a man, but it was never clear what the reporting lines were, other than to the leader. Under Paddy's leadership, a Campaigns and Communications Committee was established as a subcommittee of the party's executive committee, with responsibility for the management of all elections: general, European and local. The chair of that committee and the committee itself morphed into the general election organisation. The strength of this structure was seamless coordination of all messaging and campaigning over the different election cycles, and clear reporting lines. Political parties have poor memories, so I fear the lessons learnt here have not been absorbed recently.

Dick Newby, now Lord Newby, and Anna Werrin, now sadly dead, provided the close liaison with the leader's office so essential in an integrated election campaign. Chris Rennard, now Lord Rennard, was the leading executive for both elections and is undoubtedly a political genius. His intricate understanding of the detail of our target seats together with his shrewd strategic grasp reinforced his legendary reputation.

In light of recent allegations against Chris Rennard
I should give some explanation as to how he arrived at the
position of power he obtained within the party.

From the start of Paddy Ashdown's leadership, Chris
Rennard was in charge of campaigns in the constituencies. He masterminded the by-election victories of the
1990s and was responsible for the strategy to concentrate
on target seats in 1997, which resulted in a big increase
in seats won, without any corresponding increase in the
national vote.

The management of a political party always involves
tricky choices. Should you appoint a chief executive or
general secretary who is basically an administrator, or
should you appoint someone with campaigning experience? The Liberal Democrats had tried both approaches.
Hugh Jones, Elizabeth Pamplin and Hugh Rickard had
been administrators, Andrew Ellis had been a campaigner
and probably only Graham Elson had been both.

After the 2001 election we had a problem. Hugh
Rickard was going and we needed to appoint a new chief
executive. Chris Rennard clearly wanted the job and my
inclination was that we should appoint a campaigner. So
we did and Chris moved to responsibility for all party
activities.

It is from this period that the allegations against him
for sexual misbehaviour relate. I have no knowledge of

what happened, as during the period that Chris reported to me nobody came forward to make a complaint. I know that this has been investigated in detail and Alistair Webster QC has produced his analysis. I cannot comment on the truth or otherwise of the allegations against Chris. I can only comment on my experience.

It is clear from the report of the independent investigation commissioned by the party leadership to review party culture and procedures that the organisation needs to set up clearer systems to ensure that similar allegations in the future are dealt with more effectively and sympathetically.

The fourth reason for our success was that in the 2005 election we were undoubtedly helped by the Iraq War. Charles Kennedy was the only political leader to oppose the war, not in a knee-jerk way, but arguing that Hans Blix, the UN inspector, should be given more time to establish whether the Saddam regime had weapons of mass destruction. But George W. Bush was determined to destroy the regime and was conscious of his electoral cycle so needed to succeed before his 2004 bid for re-election. Tony Blair decided to support him. We were aware of the unpopularity of the war with a number of Labour Members of Parliament and were able to secure the defection of Brian Sedgemore, who had been the Labour Member from Luton West from 1974 to 1979 and Hackney South & Shoreditch from 1983. Brian had always been publicly associated with the Bennite wing of the Labour Party – indeed, he had been Parliamentary Private Secretary to Tony Benn for a period – and was standing down in the election.

I had known Brian for a long time; in his early years he had been a member of the Liberal Party. He was clearly disillusioned with the Labour government, not only over Iraq but also over what he perceived as their agenda to attack civil liberties. Colin Brown of *The Independent* newspaper had the story and agreed to run it on the front page if we let him have an exclusive. So Brian joined us and campaigned for us, particularly in seats where we were targeting Labour.

Brian was very welcome as a recruit, although I suspect Charles Kennedy's description of his defection as 'a pivotal moment in the election campaign' was an exaggeration.

So, clearly, we were well positioned to attract voters for whom the Iraq War was a determining factor, and won fourteen seats from Labour, although interestingly made no real headway in seats with a significant Muslim population. Some pundits felt that this result was disappointing as some colleagues had talked of winning 100 seats, which Chris Rennard and I felt was totally unrealistic.

We also failed in our attempt to unseat Tory bigwigs Michael Howard, Theresa May, Tim Collins, David Davis and Oliver Letwin, in what the press called our decapitation strategy. Tim Collins was our only scalp, in

Westmorland & Lonsdale. Ironically, Tim Collins had taken £50 from me in the 2001 election. I was on a radio programme and, rashly, was incited by the compère to bet Tim Collins £50 that Tim Farron would win his seat. Tim Collins later disclosed that he spent my £50 on a video recorder. Although encouraged to do so again in 2005, I did not repeat my bet. I bumped into him in a restaurant recently and he told me that he had no intention of returning to politics. Of course, Tim Collins's major role in political history was when working for John Major in 1993. John Major had made his now infamous 'Back to Basics' speech, contrasting the relationship between the individual and the state. Tim briefed the press that the speech referred to personal morality, which gave them the green light to investigate the personal lives of Tory Members of Parliament, with adverse consequences for the Tories in the 1997 election. Bearing in mind the later revelations of John Major's relationship with Edwina Currie, clearly the Prime Minister cannot have intended to raise the question of the personal morality of politicians!

Amusingly, a personal reaction from one of our targets whom we had failed to unseat occurred the week after the election. I was sitting having a drink with a friend in the Pugin Room in the Houses of Parliament, with my back to the door. I suddenly felt someone behind me put what seemed like a thick hood over me. I fought to take it off and realised that the person behind me was holding a jacket over me. I struggled to release myself and turned to see David Davis standing there grinning. 'That's what I think of your decapitation strategy, Tim.'

A fifth reason for our growth was that I was determined that we should be aspirational as a party. I was fed up with being involved in so many election campaigns where we were clearly planning to come third. I remember making a speech in 2003 arguing that our aim should be to ensure that when Labour became unpopular, as they inevitably would, voters would come to us as the alternative rather than the Tories. I argued in party committees for a three-election strategy, with the aim of us being in government by 2010. It of course happened, but not quite in the way I intended.

Finally, a crucial aspect of our growth was the impact of Charles Kennedy. Charles was born in Inverness and brought up in Fort William in the Highlands of Scotland. Educated locally, he went on to Glasgow University, where he was active in student politics. After Glasgow he went to the United States to study for a further degree in Indiana on the speeches and writings of Roy Jenkins. When he was in the United States he was nominated as SDP candidate for Ross, Skye & Inverness West, now Ross, Skye & Lochaber after boundary changes. In the 1983 election he surprisingly won the seat and became a Member

of Parliament at the age of twenty-three. When told of
Charles Kennedy's victory, David Owen is reputed to
have asked, 'Charles who?' In one of life's ironies, Charles
moved from studying Roy Jenkins's speeches and writings in Indiana to sharing an office with him in the Palace
of Westminster.

Charles became close to David Owen during the 1980s
when the influence of the SDP contracted after failing to
make their hoped-for breakthrough in the 1983 election.
In the 1987 election the SDP was reduced to a handful of
seats and the majority of SDP members voted for a merger
with the Liberal Party. Much to David Owen's annoyance,
Charles supported the merger and did not join Rosie Barnes
and John Cartwright in following Owen into the rump SDP.
Charles's career in the Liberal Democrats thrived and when
Ian Wrigglesworth, now Lord Wrigglesworth, stood down
as president of the party, Charles was elected and was president for the maximum permitted period of four years. On
Paddy Ashdown's resignation, Charles was the favourite to
succeed him, and once Menzies Campbell decided not to
stand, his victory was assured.

Charles was from the start a charismatic speaker. His
abilities also translated to the television interviews where
he was able effortlessly to deliver the required sound bite.
Before he became leader he often appeared on television
comedy shows, which undoubtedly increased the public's

knowledge of him when he became leader. I strongly argued that these 'soft' opportunities were good for him and he is still the only party leader who has submitted himself to the barbs of Ian Hislop and Paul Merton on *Have I Got News for You*. In opposition, Charles had developed strong friendships both with Westminster political journalists – which stood him in good stead as leader – and with political colleagues. He even went on the parliamentary rugby tour of South Africa, where he met Nelson Mandela at a reception in the presidential palace. He was somewhat surprised to be introduced to the President by team captain Lord Redesdale as Nigel Kennedy, and even more so when the President replied that he had always enjoyed his violin playing.

Charles also has strong leadership skills. Leading a Liberal Democrat political party is not easy, but during Charles's leadership the Liberal Democrat MPs invariably ended up in the same lobby voting the same way. Watching how he achieved this over a number of years, I realised that his skill was to invite a potential rebel to see him, to listen while the individual explained his concerns, and not say much, thereby giving the individual the impression that he really agreed with him but political realities were pulling us the other way. It invariably worked. This meant that in electoral terms we were not seen as a party all over the place on issues, which had often been the case in the past.

Above all, Charles had impeccable judgement as a leader on the issues of the day. The best example of this is the stance he took on the second Iraq War. It is easy with hindsight to think that his decision to oppose the war was obvious. The Labour and Tory establishments were in favour of the war and tempers were running high against those in opposition. Charles was upset when Nicholas Soames called him a traitor at a private dinner. But he stuck to his guns and the world would now say he was right.

Charles Kennedy resigned as leader in January 2006, acknowledging his problems with alcohol. Clearly, in the days of the 24-hour news cycle, alcohol consumption is harder for a senior politician to manage successfully than it was for Asquith, Churchill or George Brown. It was impossible to work closely with Charles and not realise that from time to time there was a problem.

There were the occasional high-profile incidents that have been well documented. The failure to appear in the House of Commons for the Budget debate; being the worse for wear at a celebration party given by Ramesh Dewan; and a rambling performance at the London School of Economics. It was the latter event in 2005 that provoked Tim Farron and Julia Goldsworthy, newly elected MPs, to begin the process that ended with a letter signed by a number of their colleagues calling for his resignation.

In my experience working with Charles, there were

long periods without any issues, interspersed with days when there clearly was. Ironically, by the time of his resignation he was prepared to acknowledge that there was a problem and undergo treatment. Alas too late for many of his colleagues.

Although at the time I accepted the public statements of colleagues that his drinking meant that he had to go, on reflection I now feel that there was more to it.

Personal ambition must never be discounted in politics. Menzies Campbell had not stood against Charles in the election to succeed Paddy Ashdown and would only be human if he regretted his decision not to stand. There had followed a period of serious illness as he fought and successfully overcame cancer. Rumblings against Charles were often dealt with by Anna Werrin in the leader's office, pointing out that with 'Ming' Campbell out of action there would be no successor acceptable to colleagues. But Ming was now recovered and clearly prepared to become leader, having spent a number of years showing loyalty to Charles.

After a few years in the job, all political leaders have made enemies. They come from those they have sacked, those who have not been given the promotion they feel they deserve and those who feel that they are excluded from the inner counsels of the leader. This perception of a leader's bunker mentality became true for Paddy Ashdown, is true for Nick Clegg and was certainly true for

Charles. So a new leader would give new hope to the dis-
affected. To this group would be added a number of the
new MPs elected for the first time in 2005 who had not
had any time to witness and appreciate the true quality of
Charles Kennedy's leadership.

But an overarching, almost overt, theme was ironically
that the election result in 2005 should have been better
and that to a considerable extent this was the leader's fault.
There were people around Ming Campbell who seemed
to believe that there were magic bullets we had failed to
fire in 2005 that would have delivered at least 100 seats.
Chris Rennard and I failed to damp down this expectation, which started publicly with statements by Mark
Oaten, the MP for Winchester. Our detailed analysis of
constituencies told us that our range was sixty to seventy.
In the end we won sixty-two. Off-the-record briefings to
journalists, starting at the traditional election-night party,
firmly lodged the missed opportunity story in the minds
of many political commentators, and became the narrative
for many colleagues.

Chris Rennard was not immune from criticism, not
because of the allegations of sexual impropriety that
emerged later, but because, very unfairly, he was felt to be
out of touch with modern campaigning techniques. The
best proof that the critics were wrong came in the 2010
election, in which neither Chris Rennard nor I had a role,

which demonstrated how notwithstanding 'Cleggmania' following Nick Clegg's brilliant performances in the televised leaders' debates, there was tremendous difficulty in converting votes into seats. In the event, we won fewer seats than in 2005.

I am not by nature a conspiracy theorist and had great difficulty in accepting that there had been a conspiracy by friends and colleagues to unseat Charles. I am afraid I changed my mind when I learnt recently from an unimpeachable source that the Joseph Rowntree Reform Trust had been induced to provide funding to the conspirators. Charles's drinking problems gave them the excuse they needed.

It is impossible to record the political process in which I was involved without describing the key role played by the media. Of course, the modern trend is to pursue interviews on the so-called 'soft' programmes. Margaret Thatcher started it with *The Jimmy Young Programme*, and an interview in *Tatler* or *GQ* is thought to be more valuable than one in *The Times* or a heavy interview on television or radio. So I was delighted that Charles Kennedy agreed to appear on *Have I Got News for You* after he became leader, which undoubtedly increased his recognition factor.

As chair of the party's election campaigns, from time to time I was invited to appear on the key political programmes, *Question Time* on television and *Any Questions?* on radio. *Question Time* is in a way more challenging as you can be seen by the viewer. In fact, I had for some reason been asked to appear on *Question Time* shortly after the 1992 election. I was up against Brian Gould for the Labour Party and Jonathan Aitken, who was a government minister. I arrived at Maidstone, exceptionally nervous, and was greeted by the producer, who told me that the only piece of advice she would give me was that I should ignore the briefing I had been given by the party and just be myself.

Her advice was more apt than I realised. The early questions were in line with my briefing from headquarters. Then came the bombshell. The question was about recent international proposals to restrict arms dealing. I was sitting next to the presenter, Peter Sissons, who had succeeded Robin Day. When the question was asked and Brian Gould was the first responder, Peter muttered to me that I should ask Jonathan Aitken what he knew about arms dealing. I had no clue about the allegations that would later swirl about Jonathan Aitken on that topic. I did know that if Peter Sissons was not prepared to ask the question, I certainly was not.

With *Question Time* you arrive before the programme starts and have drinks in the green room. The ability of participants to subdue their nerves with alcohol is wonderful to observe. I found a glass or two of wine before the programme calmed my nerves and loosened my tongue. Others seemed to thrive on rather more.

Over the years I appeared with a number of different panellists. Theresa May was an up-and-coming Tory Member of Parliament. She never stayed for the dinner the BBC gave panellists after the programme and clearly had no time for me – I suppose not surprisingly as we were trying to unseat her in Maidenhead. I appeared several times with Janet Daley, the journalist, whose views were as right-wing on air as they were in print. Clare Short, then a government minister, was always friendly. I was not surprised when she fell out with the Labour government over the Iraq War.

The most extraordinary performance I witnessed came from another journalist, Bruce Anderson. We were appearing with the Labour minister Beverley Hughes, who had been criticised in the press for Home Office inefficiencies regarding the processing of applications for residence in the United Kingdom. In the green room before the programme Bruce suggested that I weighed in strongly against her if the question came up. He felt that it was not his place to do so, for some reason. The question was asked and I was sympathetic to her as she had clearly been let down by her officials. Bruce tore into her in a tirade of aggression. When I said to him afterwards that I thought he was going to go easy on her, he replied that he had!

Any Questions? on the radio is different. In format there is no audience participation, unlike *Question Time*, except for the occasional request for a show of hands by the presenter Jonathan Dimbleby, who reports the result to the listeners. Unlike *Question Time*, dinner is served before the programme so you have the chance to meet and chat to your fellow panellists about the questions that are likely to come up. My most fascinating conversation was with Colin Blakemore, the scientist. Heavily involved in research to cure the diseases that affect the nervous system – Parkinson's disease, Alzheimer's disease and motor neurone disease – he was optimistic that significant progress would be made in palliative and even curative treatment in a relatively short time span.

Alan Duncan, the Tory Member of Parliament, was fun. Michael Howard had just resigned as Tory leader and Jonathan Dimbleby asked Alan on air whether he would stand for the leadership. Alan's answer was coy, so I fanned the flames by saying I thought he would be excellent. Alan blushed, not that it mattered on radio, and asked if I wanted to be his campaign manager!

I appeared twice on *Any Questions?* with Hazel Blears, the Labour government minister. On the first occasion she arrived in the hall with piles of paper, which she rifled through for an answer to each question. Clearly, she was nervous that she would go beyond the government briefing she had received. On the second occasion, a few years later, she appeared without notes. Her performance on the second occasion was much better than the first. After the programme I told her of the advice I had been given all those years ago before my first appearance on *Question Time*. She told me that she had come to the same conclusion herself.

The role of the political commentator should not be underestimated. For the politician, the demands of the broadcast media are different from those of newspapers. The ability to compress political ideas into short sound bites is essential, as, apart from big set-piece interviews, two minutes is often the maximum time available. In recent years the practice has developed that after an interview the political editor is asked to comment on the leader's remarks. So the political adviser needs to develop relationships with political editors to explain and often amplify the leader's views.

Polling shows that the majority of the electorate still obtains their political news from BBC News, so the relationship with the BBC political editors was crucial. During the Kennedy years, Andrew Marr and then Nick Robinson filled that role. I found both fair to deal with and balanced in their coverage, although Andrew did not have the same degree of rapport with Charles Kennedy as he had with Paddy Ashdown. I never agreed with the Labour attack on Nick Robinson as being pro-Tory because he had been a Tory in his youth. When I got to know him he revealed to

me once that far from being pro-Tory, whenever he interviewed any of the three leaders he saw the point they were
making. I also had close dealings with John Sergeant at
ITN, Adam Boulton at Sky News and Elinor Goodman
at Channel 4. They all treated us fairly but, as always in
those days, the challenge for us was to obtain coverage as
the third party in any political story.

Once a general election campaign had begun, the
broadcasting rules meant that the Liberal Democrats had
to be given a fair share of television and radio coverage.
Until recently the early-morning leader's press conference was a vital part of general election planning, with the
objective of setting the day's political agenda on issues we
wished to discuss.

In 2001 and 2005 the leader's press conferences were
covered on the BBC by Anthony Howard, with whom
I developed a good relationship.

Anthony Howard had been editor of the *New States-
man* in the 1960s and had then become a senior journalist
at *The Observer*, where, much to his irritation, he did not
become editor. The esteem in which he was held by a
number of his protégés who went on to great things was
evidenced at his funeral. After *The Observer* he built a
career in television, hence his role covering the leader's
press conferences.

Anthony was always fair, even if he could never quite

hide his left-leaning Labour views, although he may well have voted Liberal Democrat in Ludlow in 2005. It has always amused me how many men of Labour Party persuasion are attracted to the Garrick Club in Covent Garden and indeed wear the distinctive tie with pride. The Garrick, of course, does not admit women members. I asked Anthony once how he could justify his membership of the Garrick Club. 'Oh, that's easy, Tim,' he replied. 'Most people's subscriptions are now paid by their firms, and as more women become in charge they'll force their colleagues to vote for a change.' The most extraordinary justification I have heard.

Anthony was the son of a clergyman and was always fascinated by ecclesiastical affairs. If you were talking to him at a party and a bishop or archbishop caught his eye he would break off the conversation at once and beard the cleric. So at his funeral in St Mary Abbots Church in Kensington, the mourners were somewhat bemused by the vicar's anecdote. Apparently, Anthony was a regular attendee at evensong on Sundays. One Sunday the vicar was on holiday and the service was taken by the curate. The curate thought he had upset Anthony, as he had sat throughout his sermon with his head in his hands. The vicar later explained that Anthony always sat like that. He always assumed it was because he was trying to make up his mind whether he believed in God.

Dealing with the print media was different. None of the tabloids took any interest in us unless there was a scandal. The *Mail* and *Express* were uniformly hostile, apart from Simon Walters at the *Mail on Sunday*, who would occasionally take a story. So we were left with attempting to obtain coverage in *The Times*, *Guardian* and *Independent*, and the *Sunday Times* and *Observer* on Sundays.

The trick was either to interest a journalist in a story or, on the big set-piece occasions such as party conferences, to try to ensure that the messages we were aiming to get across were understood and hopefully mentioned in the relevant article. Martin Ivens in the *Sunday Times* and Don MacIntyre in *The Independent* were always receptive, as were Patrick Wintour in *The Guardian* and Andrew Rawnsley in *The Observer*, who tended to hunt as a pair when entertaining politicians to lunch. Peter Riddell often gave us good coverage in *The Times*, as did Greg Hurst.

During the Kennedy era, *The Times* was also our newspaper of choice for planting stories, primarily through the relationship I had developed with Tom Baldwin, then a political journalist, now working in Ed Miliband's office. The unspoken understanding was that if we gave him an interesting story as an exclusive he would run it on the front page. This worked pretty well for a number of years, but went slightly wrong after the 2005 election. We concocted a plan in the leader's office that I would leak an internal memo from me to Charles that after our good result Charles should take every opportunity to behave as a potential Prime Minister, not as leader of a third party. *The Times* duly ran the story on the front page, but surprisingly Tim Hames rubbished the document on an inside page and the general impression was given that I was criticising the leadership – which had not been the intention at all.

The relationship between journalists and politicians is symbiotic. Each side needs the other and spends time together in a social context, usually in bars or restaurants. So, inevitably close friendships do develop.

John Harrison was the first journalist with whom I developed a rapport. He lived in the borough of Richmond and helped us behind the scenes with our leaflets for council elections.

A colleague on the council had invited us both to a party and instructed us to come in fancy dress. I have always hated fancy dress and discovered that John did too. We decided to go with me as Cinderella and John as the wicked stepmother. My elegant dress and blonde wig contrasted beautifully with his short dress and hairy legs. We were never invited again.

Early in our relationship I went to a dinner at his house and met for the first time Robert Kilroy-Silk, then the Labour MP for Knowsley North, probably the most impoverished constituency in the country. He spent the evening explaining how the Militant Tendency were making his life impossible, as they were for many Labour MPs until Neil Kinnock ensured their expulsion from the Labour Party. When Robert said he had to leave to go back to his house on the Thames, I asked him if he lived in Knowsley. 'Certainly not,' was his response. 'You have obviously never been to Knowsley.' After he left, John and I agreed that it was no surprise that he was under attack by the Militant Tendency.

Tragically, John went as a BBC correspondent to South Africa during the 1980s and was killed in a car crash. Many of us suspect that this was no accident but the deliberate action of the apartheid regime.

It was at the dinner with Robert Kilroy-Silk that I first met Anthony Bevins, who became a close friend. When I knew him, Tony worked for *The Independent*, then the *Daily Express*, from which he resigned on Richard Desmond's purchase as he disapproved of Desmond's ownership of the magazine *Asian Babes*.

Tony's father had been Reginald Bevins, who had been a member of Harold Macmillan's Tory government. He was MP for Toxteth in the days when Liverpool elected Tory MPs through the votes of the Protestant working class. Inevitably, Tony tried not to show political bias but it was clear that he felt his father had been treated badly

by the 'snobs' and 'aristocrats' in the Tory Party so had
difficulty suppressing his anti-Tory feelings.

Tony was enormous fun as a companion, particularly
at party conferences, where we burnt much midnight oil
together. I learnt early in our relationship not to com-
pliment him on his tie, as he had the endearing habit of
presenting it to you. Even so, I had a cupboard full of
Bevins's ties.

Tony was always chasing stories and loved to obtain
an exclusive. When given one, he exuded bonhomie. But
when the story was given to someone else his anger could
explode. When Paddy Ashdown's office decided to give
the story of the MP Peter Thurnham's defection to the
Liberal Democrats to the *Sunday Times*, his explosion
of wrath must have been heard throughout the Palace of
Westminster.

Tony died suddenly in Slough hospital in the same
week as his wife Mishtu, from whom he was estranged
yet to whom he remained close. So his children became
orphans, virtually overnight. Mishtu was clearly a loveable
eccentric. Gail Rebuck was married to Philip Gould, Tony
Blair's pollster, and was undoubtedly the best-known figure in publishing. I was tickled when, at the wedding of
Rosie Boycott, then the editor of the *Daily Express*, Mishtu
asked Gail in all innocence what she did for a living.

Tony's funeral was attended by half the Labour Cabinet

and many friends, for all of whom a light had been extinguished by his death.

All political leaders have to absorb foreign policy, and journalists already have a role based more in influencing views than in giving the leader publicity. No journalists have been more enmeshed in foreign policy than John Simpson and Marie Colvin.

John Simpson was my contemporary at school and our paths have crossed from time to time since he rose to fame and success in the BBC. John has never really exhibited an interest in domestic politics, as was graphically demonstrated to me at the Liberal Party conference in Llandudno after the creation of the alliance between the Liberal Party and the newly formed SDP. This was the conference where David Steel made his famous speech urging representatives to return to their constituencies and prepare for government. The Thatcher government was at that stage coming third in opinion polls and the media had descended en masse on a Liberal Party conference, probably for the first time ever. Bars at party conferences are a hive of activity and conversation between politicians and journalists. John Simpson sat throughout silently reading a book. Party politics was not his bag.

Marie Colvin was hugely influential at the *Sunday Times*, particularly on the Middle East. She became close to Yasser Arafat and indeed was commissioned to write his biography, which somehow never appeared. Muammar Gaddafi, dictator of Libya, was someone else to whom she became close. Indeed, she obtained one of the last interviews with Gaddafi before his overthrow. Marie was always amused at Gaddafi's attempt to make a pass at her by reaching across and trying to turn off her tape recorder when she sat down for her interview in his desert tent. She was even more amused later on when his affections had clearly shifted as he begged her to give him Madeleine Albright's mobile number.

Marie did not agree with the stance we were taking on the second Iraq War as she was persuaded that the invasion would be welcomed by the oppressed Iraqi people with open arms. She later came round to the view that the United States had botched the reconstruction period after the overthrow of Saddam Hussein. Marie's initial views about people or events were not always correct, as was indicated by her interview with Julian Assange. When the storm broke around him he lay low in the country house of the owner of the Frontline Club. Marie obtained an exclusive interview for the *Sunday Times* and was initially impressed with his case. She changed her mind when her piece appeared in the paper. The arch-exponent of freedom of information was outraged, for some reason, that she had disclosed his negotiation for an advance on a book.

It is for her personal bravery that Marie will be best

remembered. She went into Kosovo from Albania, where,
she told me, she saw her first dead body. She covered
the Chechen civil war and escaped over the mountains to
Georgia by the skin of her teeth. She was the first journalist to interview the leadership of the Tamil rebels in Sri
Lanka and lost an eye when fired on by government forces.
She witnessed at close hand the action of British troops
led by General David Richards, now Lord Richards, in
Sierra Leone. She undoubtedly saved hundreds of lives
in East Timor when she stayed behind after other journalists had left and continued broadcasting as Indonesian
troops invaded. Tragically, she lost her life in 2012 in Homs
in Syria when she was clearly targeted by the Assad regime.
Without the bravery of people like Marie, the world would
never know the truth about conflicts from the front line.
She became my close friend and I miss her dreadfully.

My serious role in electoral politics ended with the
departure of Charles Kennedy as leader, but of course the
result of the 2010 election brought the party into government for the first time in peacetime since 1922.

David Laws and Andrew Adonis have both written
books giving their perspective on the negotiations that
followed the 2010 election, where no party won an overall
majority. I cannot comment on the details of the negotiations but I had a peripheral role as a member of the party's
national executive committee, which met daily during the

negotiations to receive reports from the negotiating team
that Nick Clegg had appointed. So my experience was
from that perspective.

Correctly, negotiations began with the Tories as they
had won more seats than Labour. It was clear from the
start that there were three choices. First, we could do
nothing; we could let the Tories form a minority government and presumably there would be another election
shortly, as had happened in 1974. Second, we could enter
into what became known as a confidence-and-supply
arrangement, under which the Tories formed the government and we agreed not to support Labour in a
no-confidence motion in the House of Commons, which
if passed would trigger another general election. In that
case we could also agree not to join Labour in voting
down the Budget each year, to ensure that the process of
government could continue. Third, we could enter into
a full coalition agreement.

At the first joint meeting of the parliamentary party
and the executive committee on the Saturday after the
election, no votes were taken, but views were expressed.
It is hard to be precise but my estimate at the time was
that 10 per cent wanted to do nothing, half preferred a
confidence-and-supply arrangement and the rest a coalition, preferably with Labour. Very few at that stage
contemplated a coalition with the Tories. Nick Clegg made

it clear that we should talk to the Tories as the largest party and that discussions should be policy driven. David Cameron had by then announced that he proposed to make a significant offer to the Liberal Democrats.

When the negotiating team reported back, it was clear that the policy discussions had gone well. I remember Andrew Stunell, the Member of Parliament for Hazel Grove, saying that he was stunned by the concessions the Tories were prepared to make to secure power.

So by Sunday the mood was shifting towards a coalition with the Tories. There was some unhappiness expressed by a number of senior colleagues. Paddy Ashdown was no longer a member of the House of Commons, having become a peer on his return from Bosnia, but as an ex-leader his views carried weight. He felt that we should not rule out an arrangement with Labour. I suspected that his views were shared by Menzies Campbell and Charles Kennedy, his successors as party leaders.

The major problem was the parliamentary arithmetic. Our votes with the Tories provided a solid working majority. Our votes with Labour did not. So Paddy asked Chris Rennard to explain that the position was not as bad as it looked. Although the two parties did not have a majority, the Irish didn't turn up and the nationalists would not vote with the Tories. It was agreed that our negotiating team should meet Labour. Whether private discussions

256256256

256256256256

had already taken place between colleagues who had links with Labour and the Labour leadership I know not.

When the team reported back their view was clear. Whatever the problems of the electoral arithmetic, there was little movement on policy issues. Labour seemed reluctant to move from entrenched positions and seemed to assume that they would continue to run the country as before, oblivious to the result of the election they had just lost. Whatever Andrew Adonis has written, our team felt that there was no real appetite in the Labour team to reach an agreement with us.

So a final meeting was convened of the parliamentary party and the executive committee to decide how to proceed. On this occasion a vote was required and, with evident reluctance exhibited by some speakers, a virtually unanimous vote approved the coalition arrangements with the Tories. The only visible vote against was from David Rendel, the former Member of Parliament for Newbury, although there may have also been some abstentions.

The coalition agreement was subsequently approved with an overwhelming vote at a specially convened party conference.

So, what conclusions can be drawn from the four years of coalition government?

First, there can be no doubt that the coalition has provided stable government, essential during a period of economic crisis. The background to the coalition negotiations had been the major crisis in the Eurozone, with the serious threat that Greece might default on its obligations, which would have serious implications for world financial stability. There can also be no doubt that the Cabinet Secretary, let alone the Governor of the Bank of England, will have encouraged the formation of a stable government.

Second, the fact that the parliamentary party and the special conference had endorsed the coalition meant that restiveness during the inevitable choppy waters has been muted. This is in marked contrast to David Cameron's problems, where a substantial minority of Tory Members of Parliament clearly blamed him for losing the election and do not approve of the coalition.

Third, the requirement to obtain the agreement of both parties to any proposal has led to proper internal discussions and inevitably produced better government. This requirement has also meant that wild policy proposals from either side are not implemented. Relationships between coalition ministers are clearly better than the Blairite–Brownite friction that so disfigured the Labour government.

Fourth, from the point of view of the Liberal Democrats there have been disappointments. The Liberal Democrat Holy Grail of electoral reform foundered when the referendum was lost. House of Lords reform also failed with the opposition of Tory members of the House of Commons.

From the political point of view, tuition fees were a disaster. The party had campaigned during the election with a pledge not to increase university tuition fees and the coalition agreement permitted Liberal Democrat Members of Parliament to abstain in any vote on the subject. When the coalition government was formed, Vince Cable was the Secretary of State for Business, Innovation and Skills, with responsibility for university education. The Labour government had commissioned Lord Browne, the former chief executive of BP, to produce recommendations. So Vince Cable and Nick Clegg had a dilemma. They could either rely on the coalition agreement, playing no role in the decision and letting the Tories implement Lord Browne's recommendations, or they could try to improve them. They opted for the latter course and made a number of improvements, particularly in ensuring that no student has to pay tuition fees while at university and starts to repay when his or her income exceeds £21,000.

As a result, the fear that students from a poorer financial background would be put off going to university has not in practice been realised. But the policy has been a disaster in political terms. The Liberal Democrats, and Nick Clegg in particular, are thought to have reneged on a solemn pledge not to increase tuition fees and have not been forgiven.

Fifth, the Liberal Democrats have clearly lost significant

electoral support. Opinion polls show our support since 2010 halving, and our local councillor base has been seriously eroded. Two clear lessons can be drawn from the May 2014 elections. In local government we are back where we were twenty years ago. Where we are well organised, and have worked the ward effectively since the previous election, we can still win. Fortunately, in many places we also hold the parliamentary seat, which bodes well for the general election in 2015. We must also realise that fighting a European election simply on European issues does not work, although an election with a turnout of only 35 per cent can hardly provide a snapshot of the views of the electorate.

What of the future? Clearly, predictions too far ahead are tricky. I remember my twelve-year-old nephew Paul Razzall asking me ten years ago which would come first – England winning the Ashes or the Liberal Democrats being in government. At the time, both seemed unlikely, but after that England won three Ashes series in a row and the Liberal Democrats are now in government.

So, have Liberal Democrats now become a regular party of government? Until 2010 the natural assumption was that the party could only really aspire to run local councils and had no real role to play nationally. Clearly, since 2010 the party has lost support from Labour voters who came to us in protest at the Iraq War. We have also lost the protest vote, some of which has gone to UKIP. As one wag put it, we need to replace people who voted for us as a protest vote because we couldn't win with people who didn't vote for us because we had no chance of winning.

Professor John Curtice, the psephologist, predicted after the 2005 election that we are moving to a situation where hung parliaments will be the norm. I agree with his analysis, even more so with the rise of UKIP. So, notwithstanding the current reduction in our support, I suspect that the political journey I began in 1967 will now leave me more often than not as a member of a party in government.

—CHAPTER ELEVEN—

THE HOUSE OF LORDS

A FTER THE 1997 election, Paddy Ashdown asked me if I would like to be nominated to the House of Lords. Before 1997, very few Liberals or Liberal Democrats had been nominated by the Prime Minister of the day – virtually none by Margaret Thatcher and only a few more by John Major. It is for the Prime Minister to decide the number to be nominated from each political party, and Tony Blair agreed ten Liberal Democrats as part of his wish to reduce the Tory domination of the Upper House.

The system of choosing life peers is clearly unsatisfactory. As Richard Holme put it succinctly, it's a question of being in the right place at the right time. We all know people with a strong record of public service who deserve to be there and are not.

Sir Nicholas Henderson (always known as Nicko, except by Margaret Thatcher, who referred to him as Nico in her memoirs) was a classic case in point. Having joined the Foreign Office in 1946, he retired from the diplomatic service in 1979 as ambassador to France and was persuaded out of retirement by Margaret Thatcher to become ambassador to the United States in 1979 when Edward Heath turned her down. Nicko had known every Foreign Secretary from the end of the Second World War well. I remember being at dinner when he was asked by the journalist Tony Howard who, in his experience, were the best and worst Foreign Secretaries. The best was easy: Ernie Bevin, because you knew he spoke with authority and would not be second guessed by the Prime Minister. The worst was surprising: Tony Crosland. Nicko felt that the art of the Foreign Secretary was to be able to deal with many different and complex issues simultaneously. He felt that Tony Crosland, although of great ability, could concentrate on only one issue at a time.

Why I was in the House of Lords and Nicko Henderson was not is beyond me.

When I joined the House of Lords in the summer of 1997, a number of major figures from the past were often there. Jim Callaghan and Quintin Hailsham were regular attenders, as was, though more infrequently, Margaret Thatcher. Roy Jenkins was the leader of the Liberal Democrat group. I had not known Roy very well, coming from the Liberal Party rather than the SDP, and I am not sure that Roy really saw the point of those of us coming into the House of Lords primarily from a local government background. I had first come across Roy in the Croydon by-election, won by the Liberal Bill Pitt in the early heady days of the alliance with the SDP. I was allocated as one of Roy's minders on a walkabout through the middle of Croydon and was staggered at his ability to charm passers-by with serious conversation without condescension.

For me, the most fascinating conversations with Roy were about his biographical work. During his time in the House of Lords he published his acclaimed biographies of both Gladstone and Churchill. He is on record as saying that when he had finished his life of Gladstone he felt that Gladstone was Britain's greatest Prime Minister, but after writing about Churchill he felt it was Churchill. His view was based entirely on the events of May 1940, when Churchill replaced Chamberlain and became head of a coalition government. According to Roy, at his first Cabinet meeting only Churchill and the Labour Cabinet members did not favour a peace deal with Hitler. After a number of Cabinet meetings, Churchill by the force of his personality changed the policy dramatically the other way. By that alone, Churchill saved us from Hitler and deserved Roy's accolade.

Sadly, Roy had died by the time a colleague of mine was wrongly arrested in Italy. In his briefcase he had a copy of Roy's life of Gladstone and a novel by Maeve Binchy. When imprisoned overnight, the life of Gladstone was confiscated as far too inflammatory and radical. Roy would have enjoyed that.

My last memory of Roy before he died is social. A pre-Christmas lunch had been organised in a pub in Wiltshire and a number of us who lived locally were invited. Arriving a little late, I found myself at the far end of the table from Roy. When offered red wine from an open bottle on the table, I turned to a member of his family and suggested she sniffed the wine as it was badly corked. 'For God's sake don't tell Roy,' she countered. 'He won't notice.' So much for the man whose enemies put it about that he was far too fond of swigging good claret.

When I came into the House of Lords in 1997, all four members of the famous SDP Gang of Four were in the House, although David Owen did not take the Liberal Democrat whip and sat as a cross-bencher. Roy stood down as leader soon after my arrival and was succeeded by Bill Rodgers. Bill has been in many ways the least high-profile of the Gang of Four, in my view without justification. To

call his autobiography *Fourth among Equals* is overmodest.
Having defected from Labour to the SDP in 1981, Bill lost
his seat in Stockton in 1983. He had spent all his life in politics, first with the Fabian Society, then as a Labour MP and
a Cabinet member under James Callaghan. I suspect that
his later job as secretary general of the RIBA was the first
time in his adult life he had ventured into the private sector.

Bill had undoubtedly been a consummate political
fixer. He had been the natural choice to negotiate the allo-
cation of seats between the SDP and the Liberals in the
run-up to the 1983 election. But when he became leader
I found his advice compelling. He asked me what I wanted
to do in the House and I replied that I had not resigned
my seat as a councillor after twenty-four years to speak on
local government. So he suggested I became spokesman
for Trade and Industry, now Business, Innovation and
Skills, which I accepted with alacrity, remaining in that
post for sixteen years before switching to spokesman for
Treasury matters.

Bill taught me how to do the job. Don't parrot party
policy but get well informed and tell the House your views.
He has the great gift of being able to communicate clear
advice in a few pithy sentences – not instructions from the
leader, but hints – and you would be a fool not to listen.

He also shared his experience as a Cabinet minister. He
told me that the trouble with ministers is that they think

they can communicate a decision and the civil service will pull the levers of power to implement it. Sadly, this is not the case, as he found particularly as Minister for Transport, where local authorities and nationalised industries held all the levers.

It was a tragedy when Bill had a stroke and had to resign as leader. But with typical resolve he fought his way back to fluency in speech, although, as he admitted to me, he still had some difficulties with subjunctive clauses!

On Bill's retirement as leader he was succeeded by Shirley Williams. Shirley is a phenomenon. Now in her eighties, her life has been varied. The daughter of the writer Vera Brittain, it is rumoured that her political career might never have started had she been chosen as the star of *National Velvet*, for which it is alleged she auditioned, instead of Elizabeth Taylor.

My main exposure to Shirley has been in election campaigns, either as chair or warm-up speaker. She is of course a brilliant speaker, in demand for any meeting for which she is available. But what is even more noticeable is the reaction of the audience. Leaving the stage with her is like walking with a rock star. People clutch at her as they would Mick Jagger or Beyoncé, and getting her out of the auditorium is a problem.

Shirley has developed a reputation for chronic lateness, although I suspect she is no later than many busy people.

I was an unwitting victim back in the 1992 general election. I was chairing a meeting in Bath, with Barry Norman, Shirley and Paddy Ashdown the speakers. There were 400 or so in the hall, who were becoming restive as we waited for Shirley to arrive. After about twenty minutes I decided to start without her and announced that I had received a message that Shirley had missed her train and would be very late, if she made it at all. Barry Norman started and after five minutes the door to the hall banged open and in marched Shirley. I gave no explanation and neither did she. But as always the audience loved her.

When Shirley retired as leader, Tom McNally was elected by the Liberal Democrat peers as her successor, the fourth leader in a row from the ranks of the SDP. Indeed, when Jim Wallace succeeded Tom as leader in 2013 he was the first ex-Liberal in that position since I joined the House in 1997.

Tom was born and brought up in Blackpool and after university in London spent a number of years working for the Labour Party in various capacities before becoming Member of Parliament for Stockport in 1979. He defected to the SDP on the formation of the party in 1981, but lost his seat as an SDP candidate in the 1983 election.

On the formation of the coalition government in 2010, Tom became a minister in the Department of Justice, as one of the first Liberal Democrat or Liberal ministers in peacetime for over eighty years. But I suspect the real high-light of Tom's political career occurred over thirty years previously when Jim Callaghan succeeded Harold Wilson as Prime Minister and Tom became head of his political office in Downing Street. Many anecdotes from this period are for Tom to tell, but my favourite was told to me not by Tom but by two retired Foreign Office diplomats on different occasions. Time and frequent repetition may have produced some embellishment or exaggeration, but the essence remains.

In the late 1970s, Greece wanted to join the European Union. At that time the major players in Europe were Germany, France and the United Kingdom, so their views were crucial. It was apparent that although there were reasons to say yes to entrench democracy in the wake of the dictatorship of the colonels, Greece was an economic basket case that could not meet the agreed financial tests for admission. At the same time, Prime Minister Callaghan was having internal difficulties in the Labour Party over Europe, notwithstanding the recent referendum confirming UK membership. In those days it was Labour not the Tories who were split over Europe. It is alleged that Tom McNally persuaded the Prime Minister that the admission of Greece would solve problems within the Labour Party, as Greece's economic difficulties would ensure that the European Union did not become as strong as the antis in the Labour Party feared.

So the Prime Minister was persuaded, but was dubious as to how France and Germany could agree. This is where the story becomes murky. It is alleged that Tom suggested that the Prime Minister should consult 'C', the head of MI6. Apparently, 'C' opined that there would be no difficulty with France as President Giscard d'Estaing had a Greek girlfriend who was withholding sexual favours à la Lysistrata until the Greek application was approved, so, as the UK and France were in favour, Germany reluctantly acquiesced.

I have never asked Tom to confirm the truth of the anecdote as I do not want to think it is untrue, in particular in light of Greece's current economic difficulties and the love life of President Hollande.

Reform of the method of appointment to the House of Lords has been on the agenda for over 100 years. Indeed, the preamble to the 1911 Parliament Act introduces curbs on the Lords' ability to block legislation emanating from the Commons as pending reform of the House of Lords.

The current system of appointment to the House takes two forms. The political appointees are nominated by the Prime Minister on the recommendation of the party leaders and are vetted as appropriate by the Appointments Commission, established in its current form by the last Labour government. Since Tony Blair was Prime Minister, the Appointments Commission has also had the task of nominating cross-benchers, the so-called 'People's Peers'.

I have no knowledge of how the 'People's Peers' are chosen, but would observe that there is not much 'people' about them. They have invariably achieved success in their adult lives and are often drawn from the traditional worlds of the law, medicine and academia. Regular nominations since the late 1990s have also massively increased the number of cross-benchers.

But my experience, particularly during my years working with Charles Kennedy, was to see at close hand how the political appointments were made. Apart from the patronage placed in the hands of the political leaders, a fundamental disadvantage of the current system is that the actual number to be nominated from each party is in the hands of the Prime Minister. Attempts have been made in recent years to make this decision more objective. Indeed, the coalition agreement in 2010 provided for appointments to be made so as to bring the political balance more in line with the result of the election. But this never really happens, as without compulsory retirement, balanced appointments would create an unmanageably large House of Lords.

Horse trading on numbers does take place. During his time as leader, Charles Kennedy always ended up with more nominations than was the starting offer. I was involved in one such negotiation in the run-up to the 2001 election.

In addition to the regular appointments by the Prime Minister, the normal convention is that when an election is called the Prime Minister appoints retiring MPs nominated by their party leaders. Although Tony Blair clearly wanted to hold an election in May 2001, foot-and-mouth disease made this impossible, and it would also prevent the council elections being held in May. So Downing Street rang Charles to ask that Liberal MPs allow the bill necessary to postpone the county council elections to June to pass without fuss. I understood that Charles had already agreed with Downing Street the list of retiring Liberal Democrat MPs to be nominated once the election was called. When he asked my advice about the postponement of the county council elections, I suggested he ask for a quid pro quo: another peerage added to the list for a retiring MP. I understand that the Prime Minister readily agreed and another name (who had better remain nameless) was added to the list, who presumably would not have become a peer otherwise.

Inevitably, the House of Lords is a political house even with the inclusion of non-political cross-benchers. Until the departure of the bulk of the hereditary peers in 1999, the House had a huge in-built Tory majority. Now the Tory, Labour and cross-bench groups are more or less equal, each group over twice the size of the Liberal Democrats.

The three political groups have a whip system, similar to that in the House of Commons, and members pretty much follow the lead set by their party leadership. There are of course exceptions. The Tories are clearly split on Europe and Labour are divided on the privatisation of the Royal Mail. From time to time, people do fall out with their parties. We have lost Hugh Thomas and Lucius Falkland to the cross-benches over the years, but neither departure was as high-profile as Matthew Oakeshott.

Matthew had been a parliamentary assistant to Roy Jenkins as Home Secretary and unsuccessfully fought a parliamentary seat in the 1970s for the Labour Party. A founder member of the SDP in 1981, he stood and lost in Cambridge in the 1983 election. Having dropped out of politics for a few years to build up his highly successful fund management business, Matthew was appointed to the House of Lords by Charles Kennedy.

Matthew is not the first politician to be obsessed by media appearances. But he did somewhat startle a meeting of Liberal Democrat peers by opining that the way to get media coverage was to single out female journalists. Most evenings he could be seen in Westminster entertaining journalists and for a number of years he was the go-to person for calling for the resignation of a Tory or Labour opponent. He was always billed as the Liberal Democrat Treasury spokesman in the House of Lords, despite the fact that Dick Newby had been the spokesman from 2000 until he became a minister in 2012.

So when he started to criticise the coalition government after 2010 and was removed by Nick Clegg as Treasury spokesman, he was probably the first politician in history to be sacked from a job he did not have. Matthew is a long-standing friend of Vince Cable, so his payment for polling in early May 2014 in various constituencies to demonstrate that Vince Cable would be a more popular leader than Nick Clegg was a serious embarrassment to Vince. Matthew has now resigned from the party and taken a sabbatical from the House of Lords. I share the view of many colleagues who agree with the statement by Liberal Democrat Justice Minister Simon Hughes at the time: 'I am clear that Matthew Oakeshott has behaved disloyally and in a way that is completely without honour in this context. It is not the time for people in the party to be seeking to undermine the party or the leadership.' Paddy Ashdown had of course threatened to castrate Oakeshott if he criticised Nick Clegg after the May 2014 elections, a threat not so far carried out, as far as I am aware.

Notwithstanding the obvious disadvantage of a system of selection based primarily on patronage once heredity is no longer the major qualification for entry, the current system does have certain advantages. An obvious example in recent years has been the ability to increase the number of people in Parliament from ethnic minority communities.

Navnit Dholakia is a classic example. During our colonial period a number of Indians, particularly from Gujarat, were sent to run the railway system in East Africa. So Navnit's father found himself settled as a station master in what was then known as Tanganyika. The young Navnit was sent to complete his education at Brighton Technical College, armed with the bowler hat that his father believed was required headwear in England and which Navnit quickly discarded.

Navnit's involvement with the Liberal Party began in eccentric circumstances. He was sitting in a Brighton pub enjoying a drink when he was approached by a young man who said that the Brighton Young Liberals were holding their annual general meeting but did not have a quorum. Would Navnit be prepared to join to give them their quorum? So he did and his political career began.

In the early 1960s Navnit was elected to the Brighton council and I suspect was subject to significant racial abuse as the National Front was on the rise. He spent a number of years working at the Commission for Racial Equality and was also involved in various capacities with the justice and prison systems. Navnit was then nominated to the House of Lords by Paddy Ashdown at the same time as me in 1997.

The president of the Liberal Democrats has a significant role to play in the party, with overall responsibility for
party rather than political organisation, and a close working relationship between president and leader is desirable.
Charles Kennedy had become leader when Diana Maddock stood down as president at the end of 1999 and there
were no obvious candidates to succeed her. Charles was
leading a delegation to Delhi to participate in the celebration of the fiftieth anniversary of the creation of the Indian
republic and Navnit had been instrumental in organising
the visit. On the Air India plane to Delhi I was sitting with
Charles and it occurred to us that Navnit would make
the perfect candidate for president. So I was dispatched
to persuade him and took him off to the galley to do so.
I suspect it was the strangest conversation the stewardess
and steward had witnessed. Indeed, I seem to remember telling him that he would have to stand all the way to
Delhi unless he agreed. He did agree and in due course
was elected as president by the party members. I did not
appreciate until later that this was the highest political
office that any member of the Indian diaspora had held
outside India, an achievement correctly recognised by the
Indian government.

After his four years as president, Navnit became deputy leader of the Liberal Democrat peers, a position he
still holds, and sat for many years on the Appointments

Commission, responsible for nominating cross-bench peers. But the titles do not themselves represent his achievements. As deputy leader he has in fact often had to deal with both collective and individual problems of the ethnic minority community, almost as if he is the Member of Parliament for the community in the United Kingdom. As a member of the Appointments Commission he ensured a suitable influx of peers from an ethnic minority background.

Although he has been recognised for his work by both the British and Indian governments, he remains one of the great unsung heroes in British politics.

The existing system of life peers also provides an opportunity to appoint people with party allegiances, who for whatever reason had been unable or unwilling to stand as an MP.

Julian Fellowes, who came into the House as a Tory peer after the 2010 election, is a good example. Julian is now the renowned creator of *Downton Abbey* but I had met him ten years previously when we appeared on BBC's *Question Time* together. In those days there were only four panellists, one from each of the three political parties and a fourth supposed independent. John Redwood, the Tory MP for Wokingham, was due to appear but with ten minutes to go had not arrived. A harassed editor appeared in the green room and asked Julian, as John Redwood had not turned up, whether for balance would he be happy to be billed as a Tory. Julian agreed but John Redwood arrived just in time.

After the usual post-recording dinner with David Dimbleby and his team, as we were in the north of England we had missed the last train. Julian and I were asked if we minded sharing a car back to London. We readily agreed and managed to secrete several bottles of BBC red wine to fortify us on our journey back to London.

The next few hours were fascinating, as Julian explained to me how he really started working. He had been an actor for some years and was appearing as Kilwillie with Susan Hampshire in the BBC series *Monarch of the Glen*. This was shot in Scotland and rather than return south between episodes he stayed in his hotel writing. He had been commissioned to write the screenplay for Robert Altman's *Gosford Park*. As we were now probably on our third bottle of red wine, I cheekily challenged him on how this could possibly work. Robert Altman was renowned for encouraging his actors to ad lib, so how could Julian be sure his script would not be ruined?

Julian gently explained that he had told Robert Altman that it would not be possible for actors playing toffs to go off-piste, so that was that. He obviously won his argument, as he carried off the Oscar the next year for his screenplay.

Julian Fellowes is not the only peer from an artistic

background. Phyllis James, more commonly known as P. D. James, the successful crime writer, was made a life peer in 1991. As she was born in 1920, her attendance these days is inevitably more limited. Andrew Lloyd Webber, the composer, takes the Tory whip, but is inevitably an irregular attender thanks to his other commitments.

That could not be said of Ruth Rendell, who became Baroness Rendell of Babergh in 1997. As Ruth Rendell she created the popular Wexford crime stories and under the pseudonym Barbara Vine she explored the unintended consequences of family secrets and hidden crimes. Ruth takes the Labour whip and despite being born in 1930 is still a regular attender. She told me last year that her regular pattern of life was to write in the morning and then walk from Hampstead to the Houses of Parliament!

Whatever the obvious deficiencies of the system of appointment, Julian Fellowes, Andrew Lloyd Webber, Phyllis James and Ruth Rendell would not be able to make the contribution they do if they had to stand for election.

When I first entered the House of Lords, hereditary peers were still entitled to attend, which meant that the House had well over a thousand members. Whatever the pros and cons of the hereditary principle I am sure that most people would regard a group in which 44 per cent were educated at Eton as somewhat narrow in outlook for modern Britain. So in 1999 the legislation to remove the hereditary peers from Parliament was passed – except for ninety-two who survive as the result of a bizarre compromise agreed by Derry Irvine and Robert Cranborne. The strangest element of this compromise is the system of by-elections when one of the ninety-two dies. The ninety-two were divided between the three parties and the cross-benchers pro rata to their number in the House prior to the cull. So the Liberal Democrats have five and Labour even fewer. When one of the ninety-two dies, a by-election is held in a constituency consisting of the surviving members of his or her party grouping. So when one of the five Liberal Democrats dies the four surviving Liberal Democrats elect his or her successor. A strange system! I would have made the ninety-two life peers.

Although clearly no modern second chamber should be based on the hereditary principle, they did often provide some amusement. I distinctly remember standing outside the chamber in 1998 waiting to vote and hearing a conversation between two hereditary peers I had never seen before.

'Hello, old boy, haven't seen you for a while.'

'Nice to see you, John.'

'So what's this vote about, buggery or badgers?'

You couldn't make it up.

Of course, a number of the hereditary peers were more serious. Conrad Russell took the Liberal Democrat whip after he became Earl Russell on the death of Bertrand, the eminent philosopher. Conrad was not a master of small talk, nor indeed always of good political judgement. His article in *The Times* when Jackie Ballard stood against Charles Kennedy for leader of the party describing her as potentially another Gladstone was not his finest hour. But on topics within his area of expertise he was fascinating. Conrad was a historian and an academic at London University specialising in Queen Elizabeth I and the Stuarts. I once asked him what he felt had been his most original piece of historical research. He felt it related to the execution of the Duke of Norfolk for treason by Queen Elizabeth. This had been engineered by her adviser Robert Cecil, the forerunner of the Salisbury family who have provided so many statesmen over the centuries. Conrad had discovered a letter written by the Duke of Norfolk to Cecil before his execution, entrusting the care of his children to Cecil, his arch-enemy.

A more personal reminiscence occurred when I found myself sitting next to him in one of the House of Lords bars. I reminded him of the occasion when, at the age of eighteen, I had sat next to his father at dinner. 'Well, Tim,' he replied, 'I hope my father behaved better to you at the age of eighteen than Gladstone did to him at the same age.' When I asked him what had happened he told me that throughout the meal Gladstone had not spoken one word to his father, until at the end of the meal he turned and asked him why he thought they were serving port in the claret glasses.

After the removal of the majority of the hereditary peers, further reform stalled until after the foundation of the coalition government in 2010. The government, very much driven by the Liberal Democrat Deputy Prime Minister Nick Clegg, produced a bill to phase out the existing members of the House of Lords and replace them with elected members. I suspect it would not have carried the House of Lords, and operation of the Parliament Act would have been necessary to pass the bill. But this was not put to the test as serious opposition from Tory backbenchers in the House of Commons forced the government to withdraw it.

I have always believed that the second chamber should be elected, but also feel that reform of the method of selection is not enough. Any reform must also address the relative powers allocated to each House.

At present, the main role of the House of Lords is to revise and improve legislation that has been passed by the House of Commons, often with inadequate scrutiny as a result of the timetabling and guillotine system operated by the government whips. The worst example in my experience was the Companies Bill in 2006, on which I led for the party in the House. This was a lengthy bill that provided a comprehensive reform of company law, but when it left the House of Commons only 50 per cent had been subject to scrutiny and the remainder passed en bloc. This is now usual for complex bills passing the House of Commons.

Although members of the House spend a huge amount of time improving bills, at the end of the day the will of the elected chamber will prevail. But if both Houses are elected, both Houses will have an electoral mandate – a recipe for deadlock unless the relative powers of both Houses are resolved in advance.

There is undoubtedly a feeling that any change in the method of selection should not damage the ambience and traditions of the House of Lords. It is certainly true that political hostility between members is less than in the House of Commons and significantly less that I had experienced in local government. The worst example for me had occurred in the run-up to the 1986 council elections. On the Friday before the election, the local paper ran a front-page story emanating from the Tories that alleged I had corruptly obtained planning permission for a company of which I was a director. In fact, I had been unaware of the application, which had been dealt with by the planning officers under delegated powers and, as I discovered later, had actually been refused. Advice from a friendly QC over the weekend told me that I had an open-and-shut libel case. He also wisely suggested that I wait to see what happened in the election. We won overwhelmingly so I did not sue, but obtained an apology from the paper. It did not endear the Tories to me.

The more civilised relationship across parties in the House of Lords leads most advocates of reform to believe that after reform the courtesies of debate in the House should be maintained. It is certainly true that notwithstanding the increased number of refugees from the House of Commons, the tone and atmosphere in the House of Lords is different. However, praise of conduct in the House can be overdone. Although there is no barracking on the lines of Prime Minister's Questions, political or personal knives are often out.

In the days when the Lord Chancellor both presided over the House on the Woolsack and then stepped to one side to speak as a government minister, Derry Irvine was introducing a bill to reform legal aid. When he was winding up I heard him tell my Liberal Democrat colleague Martin Thomas, who is a QC, that if he looked at the 1997 Labour Party manifesto, nowhere in it would he find any reference to the preservation of his income.

Baroness Blatch's rudeness was in a different league. For some reason, Emily Blatch felt her role in politics was to put her finger in the dyke to oppose all the sexual reforms of the Blair era. I remember on one occasion she rose to respond to Lord Annan in a debate about gay rights.

Lord Annan was an eminent academic and ran King's College, Cambridge.

'I can never quite remember,' she sneered, 'whether the noble Lord is from King's or Queens' College.' Not exactly courteous and obviously a gay smear.

But by far the rudest and most arrogant comment I witnessed came earlier in my time in the House, from Lord Beloff. I had come across Max Beloff as a young man at Oxford at a dinner for undergraduates from St Paul's School. Apart from Tom Howarth, the High Master, the guests of honour were Isaiah Berlin and Max Beloff, both Old Boys of the school. It was Isaiah Berlin of whom Maurice Bowra, Warden of Wadham College, memorably said, 'Isaiah is like our Lord Jesus. He talks a lot but doesn't publish much.' He certainly talked a lot at our dinner. Max Beloff said little except to tell me, after I had made a naive speech of welcome to the guests, that if I wanted to get on in life I would need to improve my speaking abilities. I was mortified at the age of twenty and that probably confirmed my decision not to go to the Bar.

Nearly forty years later, Max Beloff had moved in the House of Lords that the government was unfair in its treatment of Oxford and Cambridge Universities. Unsurprisingly, the heavyweights of the Oxbridge establishment lined up in support of his motion and the only two against him were Tessa Blackstone, the minister, and Lord Desai, an academic at the London School of Economics. In winding up the debate, Max Beloff told Lord Desai that had he had the benefit of an Oxbridge education he would have better marshalled his argument.

So Max Beloff had not changed since humiliating me forty years previously, but I felt smug satisfaction in having proved him wrong in the paths I had taken in life.

So, will we see reform of the House of Lords in my lifetime?

I suspect not if that means major change. First, the issue of the powers of a reformed House of Lords, which I touched on earlier, remains a formidable obstacle. Second, a sizeable number of members of the House of Commons will be reluctant to give an elected mandate to peers. Third, the principle of turkeys not voting for Christmas will apply, so the House of Lords will not pass a bill that removes existing peers. Although the Parliament Act could be used to ultimately pass the legislation, what future government would want its legislative timetable bogged down on an issue about which the public appear uninterested?

EPILOGUE

S
O, WHAT CONCLUSIONS do I draw from the
events I have described?

Clearly, luck has played a considerable part.
It is now generally accepted that children flower best if
shown love during their first two years. Before my father
returned from the war I was showered with love both by
my mother and her sister, Thora, from which I have ben-
efited hugely. I was lucky with my education at St Paul's
School and Oxford in the 1960s, which gave me an unri-
valled intellectual grounding. I was lucky in the timing
of my birth. When I was an undergraduate, Oxford University still played cricket against the counties, so I could
test my abilities against the best. I was lucky that when

I became a solicitor the hours were still those of a 'gentle-man's profession'. Office hours were 9.30 a.m. to 5.30 p.m. and nobody stayed beyond 6 p.m. This meant that once I was elected to Richmond Council I could leave the office at 6 p.m. and be at the town hall for committee or council meetings well before the 7 p.m. appointed start. It never occurred to me that I needed permission to be a councillor. Colleagues went to the pub after work; I went to a council meeting. Partners were also encouraged to become direc-tors of client companies, as long as the fees went into the firm. So I was able to develop my love of business, which enabled me to move from the law in 1995.

None of what I did in politics or business would have been possible today. Corporate lawyers in major law firms are working twelve-hour days, often with weekend require-ments, so local politics would be impossible. Following the development of corporate governance restrictions, most law firms prohibit partners becoming directors of client companies, to avoid perceived potential conflicts of inter-est. So both of the external avenues I pursued would have been impossible had I been born twenty-five years later.

Clearly, some of the people I have described as meet-ing through chance encounters became friends, but I have also been lucky in the family, friends and colleagues who have been with me on my journey through life – not just chance encounters, but the unsung heroes and heroines of my experiences whom I have chosen not to embarrass by including. But I cannot avoid mentioning two: John Mitchell, who established a corporate finance business with me in 1995 and sadly died in 2006, and Danelle Filce, who joined me from Frere Cholmeley nineteen years ago and without whose loyal support, dedication and friendship I could not have achieved what I have.

So throughout the many different paths my life has taken, I have been loyally supported by family, friends and colleagues. I have always felt sorry for people who have spent their lives driven by ambition, often not resulting in a happy outcome. As St Theresa memorably opined, 'There are more tears shed over answered than unanswered prayers.' So the common factor in any success I have had, as I hope the reader has realised, is best described by Reba J. Hoffman: 'Never underestimate the benefit of chance encounters.'

INDEX

Note: the following abbreviations are used in the index:
TR = Tim Razzall and LD = Liberal Democrats